TALKING WITH CATS

TALKING WITH CATS

A Journey of Spirit, Healing and Wisdom on the Camino de Santiago

W. LEE NICHOLS

BALBOA
PRESS
A DIVISION OF HAY HOUSE

Copyright © 2013 W. Lee Nichols.

All rights reserved. No part of this book may be used or reproduced by any means, graphic, electronic, or mechanical, including photocopying, recording, taping or by any information storage retrieval system without the written permission of the publisher except in the case of brief quotations embodied in critical articles and reviews.

Author photograph by Tina Nichols-Murillo

Balboa Press books may be ordered through booksellers or by contacting:

*Balboa Press
A Division of Hay House
1663 Liberty Drive
Bloomington, IN 47403
www.balboapress.com
1-(877) 407-4847*

Because of the dynamic nature of the Internet, any web addresses or links contained in this book may have changed since publication and may no longer be valid. The views expressed in this work are solely those of the author and do not necessarily reflect the views of the publisher, and the publisher hereby disclaims any responsibility for them.

The author of this book does not dispense medical advice or prescribe the use of any technique as a form of treatment for physical, emotional, or medical problems without the advice of a physician, either directly or indirectly. The intent of the author is only to offer information of a general nature to help you in your quest for emotional and spiritual well-being. In the event you use any of the information in this book for yourself, which is your constitutional right, the author and the publisher assume no responsibility for your actions.

*Any people depicted in stock imagery provided by Thinkstock are models, and such images are being used for illustrative purposes only.
Certain stock imagery © Thinkstock.*

Some names have been changed in this book to protect the privacy of the individuals involved

*ISBN: 978-1-4525-7550-6 (sc)
ISBN: 978-1-4525-7552-0 (hc)
ISBN: 978-1-4525-7551-3 (e)*

Library of Congress Control Number: 2013910085

Printed in the United States of America.

Balboa Press rev. date: 06/20/2013

For my grandchildren, with all my love
Harper Nichols ~ Christopher Bryant ~ Nicole Bryant
Live your truth. Express your love. Take your journey.

Table of Contents

Prologue ix

Part 1 ~ the Pilgrimage 1

   1 - Forgiveness 3
   2 - Kindness 15
   3 - The Borgia Legacy 23
   4 - A Woman Alone 31
   5 - Hanging the Innocent 39
   6 - Talking With Cats 49
   7 - Pit of Bones 55
   8 - Alive & Well 63
   9 - Suffering is optional 73
   10 - Demons on the Riverbank 77
   11 - The Roman Road 87

Part 2 ~ the Awakening 97

   12 - Festival in Leon 99
   13 - Companions 117
   14 - Land of the Maragato 125
   15 - Wild Dogs of Foncebadón 131
   16 - Ways of the Way 141
   17 - Mountain of Mist 149
   18 - Ambushed by a Horse 157
   19 - Confession & Compassion 165
   20 - The Inner Child 173
   21 - March to Glory 181
   22 - La Fachada 191

Part 3 ~ the Odyssey 199

23 - Santiago de Compostela.. 201
24 - Finisterre, the End of the (Known) World 205
25 - Murcia (Muxia), Synchronicity and Flow 215

A Note to the Reader 223
Gratitudes & Acknowledgements 225
Resources.. 227
Bibliography... 229

Prologue

If you follow your bliss, you put yourself on a track,
That has been there all the while, waiting for you,
And the life you ought to be living is the one you are living.
~Joseph Campbell

"You have prostate cancer, probably stage four, we will have to operate soon," announced Dr. Jamie Wong of the prestigious Jenkins Clinic in Atlanta Georgia. Perhaps I had been in denial, hoping for an alternative cure other than radiation, chemotherapy or surgery, something I never wanted to consider. Perhaps it would not exist if that word were not said. That word "cancer" would define my future and hold me in its prison for the coming weeks.

We humans, like all life and energy in the cosmos, are subject to dynamic change and chaos in our lives. It can descend quickly and often with little warning and then it appears we are caught in a downward spiral so dramatic there is no escape. When that happens we are deposited in a foreign and barren landscape with no clues and no maps to find our way home. I had been caught in one of those spirals of chaos when the great financial disaster of 2008 sucked my business, home, possessions and identity into its black hole of bankruptcy and loss. Now, still struggling to stabilize, I had cancer.

After surgery, my doctors wanted to begin radiation immediately. "No, I will not. Instead, I want to do something that will send a message to every cell in my body that it's not over yet."

"Then what is it that you want to do?" Dr. Wong asked.

"I am going to walk five hundred miles across Spain," I blurted out. I had no idea just when or how long that idea had been hatching in my head.

I explained the story of pilgrimage on the Camino de Santiago (the Spanish pilgrim's road to Saint James), how much I enjoyed walking, that I was a history buff and a foodie with a chef's background. I felt an urge of defiance and purpose beginning to form within my spirit, but passed off the pilgrimage to others as possibly "My Last Adventure."

The concept of pilgrimage had always appealed to me. Perhaps now that I reflect on the idea, my whole life has been in preparation for an adventure of the inner quest. Ambrose Bierce is credited with saying, "A pilgrim is a traveler that is taken seriously." Now I would be taking my pilgrimage seriously—I would no longer be a traveler cloaked in tourist clothes. I was ready to take ownership of my journey.

I entered the camino in the spring of 2012 with the resolution that I would heal from the many scars and emotional wounds I had carried throughout life. I knew that I would have to face my fears and challenges with honesty and a willingness to accept the truth. The desire and commitment to find an authentic life became the key to open a secret world, hidden within my soul. Fears and demons had ruled my life from padlocked cells in the darkest of dungeons since childhood.

Starting in Pamplona, Spain, I walked 450 miles on the camino to reach Santiago de Compostela in sixty days. Every day became my teacher as the culture, myth, history and fellow pilgrims led me on a quest of acceptance, wisdom and truth.

Mysterious and truly magical forces of flow and awareness emerged to guide me along the pilgrim's way. The towns of Santiago, Finisterre and Murcia took over the remaining thirty days of my journey. I was awakened to revelations of empowering insights and spiritual truths that were lessons in humility, mindfulness and nature. This pilgrimage became my greatest teacher as places, persons and events took me on an odyssey of life-changing proportions. "There are only two mistakes one can make along the road to truth; not going all the way and not starting." ~Buddha

Part One
The Pilgrimage

All that we are is the result of what we have thought.
If a man speaks or acts with an evil thought, pain follows him.
If a man speaks or acts with a pure thought, happiness follows him,
Like a shadow that never leaves him.
~ Gautama Buddha

1

FORGIVENESS

There is almost a sensual longing for communion
With others who have a large vision.
The immense fulfillment of the friendship between those engaged
In furthering the evolution of consciousness
Has a quality impossible to describe.
~Pierre Teilhard de Chardin

At six a.m., one hundred fourteen pilgrims put their feet on the floor of the seventeenth century Jesuit Church of Jesús y María as though a bell or alarm had simultaneously shook them out of their bunks. Actually, no alarms had sounded; most of these pilgrims had been on the Camino for a week or more and were now responding to their internal awareness of time. I soon discovered that sleeping pilgrims respond en mass to the faintest rustle of a sleeping bag or the crackle of plastic being shoved into a backpack. It is not considered cool to set one's iPhone or watch—after all; we are on a medieval pilgrimage.

We were cocooned into the old Jesuit church's modern addition, where sleeping quarters had been sandwiched into the side naves of the ancient stone building. The spotless, sparse elegance of stone, brick and gleaming hardwood gave warmth and a surrealistic contrast to the neat rows of double bunks. I was more than excited to begin my first day on the camino and joined the fray for the bathroom, getting dressed and double-checking backpacks. After hurried farewells to new friends, I was soon in pursuit of coffee and crescents.

I had decided to forego the traditional pilgrimage start in the French town of St. Jean Pied De Port. Instead, I avoided the treacherous trek through the Pyrenees and today I would begin on their western slope in Pamplona, Spain. I had been following the pilgrim's blog online to learn that there was still some snow and hazardous conditions on the mountains—too difficult for my unstable beginning. I was just cutting fifty miles from the normal pilgrimage, a mere ten percent of a five hundred mile adventure.

Bronze scallop shells embedded in the sidewalks marked the exit out of Pamplona to direct us into the countryside. Though it was only 7 a.m., the bulk of pilgrims from most of the hostels in Pamplona were well ahead of me; some were already on the mountain with the plan of walking thirty-five to forty km. that day. Many seem to always be in a hurry and pay little attention to relaxing over breakfast or a mid-day repast featuring the *comida del dia* (meal of the day). They snack on the run, grab a sandwich or pastry, quickly washed down with coffee, soda or beer. It is sad but true that the majority do not allow sufficient time for the camino to become their friend and guide.

It has many stories to tell, but like all worthy tales, we must stop and listen. Largely due to the limits of jobs and family, modern pilgrims try to cram a five or six week walk into much less time. Instead, I had chosen to take eight weeks with a buffer zone of four more weeks at the end, should I need it. I had only 721 km. (about four hundred fifty miles) remaining to reach Santiago de Compostela.

The camino took me though two city parks and the University of Navarra campus before crossing the Rio Sadar on a stone bridge. A short walk led to the affluent village of Cizur Menor, an upscale bedroom community and dorm town. I encountered only polite, well-groomed dogs, manicured lawns and flower gardens with roses trailing on fences. Lovely, but not what I expected to experience on this journey.

Talking With Cats

Fortunately for my expectations, the road soon led onto a dirt path that opened to a beautiful vista of farms and rolling land, at the end of which stood the Alto del Perdon. The "Mount of Forgiveness" is only a mere hill of 790 meters or 2590 feet, but it didn't earn its name without justification. Today, it stood defiant, looming large in the morning sun, challenging my ascent and pathway to the west. It did not look like a place of forgiveness.

The trail up the mountain soon became a narrow gutter, filled with rocks that seemed to always be on the move. I found climbing a struggle, which accelerated quickly to just plain suffering. My left knee and right hip were acting like they needed to be replaced. Every part of my body was reporting in with complaints and protest; the shoulders and back were already in the red zone of alerts. I had worked hard to reduce the contents of my backpack and the twenty-two pounds that I now carried were non-negotiable. The incline and frequent switchbacks didn't allow for much relief while the ditch remained narrow, dusty and rock infested.

I decided that defeat was not an option and that I was going to Santiago even if I had to crawl. That was actually a good idea; I leaned over my two trekking poles and became a sweaty, four-legged old man with a mission.

Suddenly, I heard the ding of a small bell behind me. A robust young cyclist was pushing his bike up that twisty, rocky gutter of a path as though he had a party to attend. He wished me *buen camino* (good road) and was soon out of sight without as much as a bead of sweat. I was surprised that the mountain had become so very difficult. After all, I had practiced on Big Glassy Mountain at the Carl Sandburg Estate in North Carolina for six months. I had arrived feeling confident about the camino. Yes, Big Glassy is only a three mile round trip but it is steep and rocky in places.

Nearing the top of what had become my Mount Everest, a row of strange other-worldly sentinels came into view. The city of Pamplona had constructed forty giant, futuristic looking windmills across the summit of old nasty. What a clever way to destroy the medieval aura of the majestic Navarran landscape, I thought. As I pulled myself up over the final outcrop of rocks, I discovered why they had chosen this place;

the wind was blowing at gale force. My hat sailed off like a flying saucer only to crash-land against the base of one of the aliens. Three very large arms started rotating faster as though he wanted to help catch my hat, but I knew it was the wind he really wanted. "Mountain, what did you say your name was?"

As I turned to see the eastern view with the majestic Pyrenees as a backdrop, another greeting loomed large and heroic in size. A wrought iron group of life-size medieval pilgrims, heads bent into the western wind, trailed along the cliff's edge. Some of the sculptures were on horseback, another lead a pack animal and they all carried tall staffs. They represent the long pageant of pilgrims that have braved the climb, the winds and perils to find their chosen paths in life. We can only imagine the hopes, prayers and dreams carried by the thousands who have passed this spot since the year nine hundred fifty. I stopped to reflect on my own journey as I read the inscription on the sculpture: *Donde se cuza el Camino del viento con el de las estrellas.* (Where the path of wind and stars meet.) The beautiful city of Pamplona lay below, spreading out to the base of the formidable Pyrenees. It was good to be at the top.

As I moved to find the trail down the western flank of the mountain, I was startled to step in front of an auto. To my surprise there was a paved highway that brought tourists up to the overlook. This was the first of what would become many reminders that I had chosen to walk the ancient path with occasional encounters of the modern kind. Before arriving on this pilgrimage, the twenty-first century was always with me and the choices I made daily were in that context. I now had a foreshadowing of the days and weeks to come as the camino would take me into the medieval landscape of unchanged villages, churches and castles of the Knights Templar and back again. This journey was about to become a time-machine of the mind and spirit.

Later on I would learn the truth of this as I crossed busy roads or looked up to see jet planes with their contrails etching signature lines in the sky. The few large cities that I entered were even more shocking with flying overpasses and aerial junctions. Sleek vehicles with darkened windows moved with high speed through mazes of concrete intersections. I knew that those inside were unaware of the stream of pilgrims below. The blur of nearby villages and the farmers who grew their food would not register as anything meaningful either. Most modern travelers had sold all the allotted time of their lives to buy a material world of possessions, luxuries, and status. Pilgrimage soon separates illusion from reality. How different the world and what we perceive, when we walk. It actually talks to us.

While carefully picking my way down the western side of the mountain, I couldn't help but reflect on its name and what it had been teaching me. Climbing the Mountain of Forgiveness on my first day walking the camino was starting to feel like more than mere coincidence.

"It's a setup for me to face that word forgiveness," I said to the raging wind.

Without any thought, I found myself asking, "Who should I forgive?"

"Yourself," the little voice in my head chimed in.

"From what," I asked. Here I was, the first day walking the Camino and I was talking to myself.

I guess that I had known the answer all along. Now with unlimited time alone on the road, I could deal with the big questions. My mind flashed on the many times in the court room of my life—how I, presiding as judge, had brought the gavel down as "Guilty" on the shrinking soul of self. There were so many people and events that I felt guilty about: the divorce, the wrong words to those I loved, the midlife crisis, the business failure, and the loss of family possessions. The list went on. Wow! I was guilty of all that and more.

How to forgive myself was strong in my thoughts as I stumbled down a rocky embankment barely catching a small dusty bush to break the fall. It was a long way down the mountain, rocky and steep, but the dirt path was much wider here, with abundant vegetation on either side. The heat and climb left me exhausted, and then I ran out of water. I trudged on, carefully picking my way while using the trekking poles to keep me steady and take pressure off the legs.

The little voice came back and buoyed me with an "aha" of thoughts about forgiveness as a virtue. In fact, this was something I was ready to consider as a pathway to becoming a more loving person. I knew of studies at universities, which confirmed that people who forgive are happier and have better overall health than those who hold resentment. There was empirical evidence that people who showed forgiveness had healthier hearts and nervous systems. It's just that until today, I didn't know that I had the problem. It was shocking to awaken to the fact that I needed to forgive myself for a lifetime of self-abuse and blame.

"What better place than on the Mountain of Forgiveness?" I thought. I was ready to surrender the pain and mend a wound in the fabric of my being. At that moment I felt as though there was a deep and bottomless hole in my soul. After all, during a few days of preparation in Madrid, I had committed to accept my own truths as they surfaced.

The small computer tablet that I carried was my camera, telephone, e-mail, flashlight, GPS locator, compass, calculator and book. Yes, I was carrying a twenty-first century gadget into the medieval past. It was also my umbilical cord to poetry, literature and the family that I loved. Before leaving for the camino, I had downloaded many favorite quotes from spiritual and philosophical idols. Now was the time to open some of the inspiration that lay waiting within my icon laden time capsule.

Near the path was an old log in the shade of a scrub oak. Here, now, I was ready to take responsibility and unconditionally love and forgive myself. One of the finest quotes that helped me most came from the wonderful Maya Angelou.

"I don't know if I continue even today, always liking myself. But what I learned to do many years ago was to forgive myself. It is very important for every human being to forgive herself or himself because if you live, you will make mistakes—it is inevitable. But once you do and you see the mistake, then you forgive yourself and say, 'Well, if I'd known better I'd have done better,' that's all. So you say to people who you think you may have injured, "I'm sorry", and then you say to yourself, 'I'm sorry.' If we all hold onto our mistake, we can't see our own glory in the mirror; we can't see what we are capable of being. You can ask forgiveness of others, but in the end the real forgiveness is in one's own self."

Her words rushed over me as though she was whispering them in my ear. They became truth evident and filled my darkness with a new light of wisdom and understanding.

Talking With Cats

We should never become so removed from the heart as to assume that the wisdom of others can't be a valuable resource. Our path stands firmly on the shoulders of those who have walked theirs. It is evolution manifest. Like the many who have left a light burning on my path, my finest hope is to do the same. The teachings of Buddha, Jesus, Mohammed, Plato, Gandhi and Martin Luther King, Jr. continue to inspire someone, somewhere every day. Many leaders of global corporations, governments, science and the arts accept their Laureate, their awards, with the humble praise for those who awakened them. With that said, I find that the key to another human's heart is a cosmic riddle. In my own case, the quote from Maya Angelou was not the first one that I read, nor was it the first time. The door to my pain was ready to be unlocked and her words had the key.

Once down the mountain, it became painfully evident that I would not be able to walk another four miles to reach Puente La Reina. The next village of Uterga would house me for the night in whatever was available. A barn actually sounded quite restful.

The camino meanders through the center of Uterga following the main street. Its white washed houses, with large stone lintels above windows and doorways, attest to the town's medieval heritage as a welcoming sanctuary for pilgrims. In front of the sixteenth century Gothic church of La Asuncion stood a large fountain, gushing forth spring water that cascaded into its stone reservoir. Two plaques in Spanish had been fastened to the fountain, pretty much at eye level. The oldest, chiseled in stone read, "Very Good Drinking Water," the second, modern but official looking, stated, "This water is natural and has not been sanitized." Well now, was that a disclaimer to heed or to ignore? I drank deeply. Another sweaty, dusty pilgrim hobbled towards the fountain as I was filing my pack's reservoir and inquired, "Is the water good?" "Delicious," I replied, "I just drank four cups."

The private hostel—Albergue Camino de Perdon (Way of Forgiveness) was housed in a handsome two story building in the next block. The doña welcomed me as she would an old friend—with assurance of a clean bed and a warm meal with some fine local wine. After a hot shower and the day's menu of salad, grilled trout with red peppers and an exquisite smooth flan, the restorative process was amazing. My knee and hip still ached but the heady Navarran wine eased the pain considerably.

Like most of the albergue on the Camino Francés, this one had Wi-Fi and I spent the afternoon on the patio journaling and connecting to friends and family. That evening I enjoyed fresh fruit and tea before exploring the small town at twilight. The fountain was the loudest sound in the village. The town stood stark and quiet with shuttered windows and no one in the streets. It was just the stars and me, standing alone in medieval Spain as though it had always been this way.

The gratitude and excitement of being on the Camino kept me awake and alert with thoughts of the past few weeks and how I had progressed from cancer surgery to plans to walk this pilgrimage across Spain. During recovery, I started by walking around a small lake, then I graduated to walking the flat trail around two mountains near my home. And so it was, each day I became stronger until I scaled four miles round trip on Big Glassy Mountain. That day, like today, I stood on the top and yelled to the world, "Yes I can."

Day two would be a short walk but a long journey back into the history of the Camino Francés. Some of the highlights I had scheduled into this pilgrimage were the historical side trips along the way. On this day it was to be Eunate, considered by many to be the most important Romanesque church in Navarra. I was in no hurry to leave Uterga since the detour to Eunate was a scant three miles on a flat country road. Early morning mist hovered over fields of poppies while lavender and wildflowers embraced the rolling earthen path. The pastoral beauty was breathtaking as one farm flowed into another with groves of almond trees outlining their patchwork design. Unlike America, there are no buildings, no houses and no signage along the country roadways—the people live in their villages.

Once again, most pilgrims had gone on, so the few stragglers left were strung down the roadway in alternating patterns of singles with a few couples and threesomes. Most were moving faster than I cared to walk and those behind me soon passed with smiles and the traditional "Buen Camino."

I arrived in the little stone village of Muruzábel, where the detour to Eunate leaves the camino. The town sits on a bluff, overlooking vast fields of irrigated farmland, most with their sprinklers on, showering jewels of mist over the new spring plantings. The church of St. Stephen sits on the main square where a pilgrim's fountain spills forth; no one was there but the birds to receive its blessing. There were clear directions in town to the Eunate detour but I saw no pilgrims on that road.

For most, the camino would be walked without detours, the most direct and expedient way to Santiago. For me, the journey was to become my teacher; it was all about the road and not a destination. The air was still misty from the powerful sprinklers that scattered rainbows in the morning sunlight as I headed down into the valley. It was puzzling that in the entire expansive vista I could see no buildings let alone an ancient stone church.

In the valley, another sign directed me toward a large grove of oak and evergreen. I soon discovered that the trees concealed a paved roadway, beyond which sat the octagonal thirteenth century mystery that I had come to see. A lone tour bus was sitting in the gravel parking lot.

The church's origins are somewhat obscure but most attribute it to the Knights Templar. They built several octagonal churches on the camino, all modeled on the Holy Sepulcher in Jerusalem. I was mystified at how the small symmetric interior could be a church; it appeared more like a location for ritual. Of the eight unadorned stone walls, six would have been for seating with the remainders for entry and altar. The structure was a veritable curiosity shop; the surrounding exterior arched wall was puzzling in its contrasts and possibilities for use. For example, delicate paired pillars support what appears to be a cloister, but it is open to the elements and in full view—on the outside of the church.

The columns are Gothic but have Romanesque capitals carved with monsters, musicians and vegetables. Others have outsized heads that are paired with musical instruments. Later on, a priest who has studied the Templars suggested to me that they used Moorish stonecutters and craftsmen.

The lone tour bus was still in the parking lot. Except for the caretakers no one seemed to be around. Frequently during my tour I would hear a low murmur, perhaps a chant. I was beginning to think that my antenna was picking up another dimension, perhaps a Templar's Mass. I was certainly open to that—but far off the mark.

A wall of perhaps one hundred feet connected the front corner of the caretakers building with the entrance gate to the church. I followed the chants around to the back of the church, where a robed figure was conducting worship service before a congregation seated on the ground. This was in the open space between the two buildings which kept them out of sight behind the fence. As I listened from my hidden vantage point, I was surprised that the chants and spoken word were not in Latin or Spanish. I had forgotten that I was still in Basque country, where their ancient tongue remains in proud usage.

I chose to catch up with the camino by taking a detour road through more irrigated fields and rolling hills covered in vineyards. At one point, powerful sprinklers were shooting storms of drenching water across the path ahead. I took great pride in being prepared for such an event by donning my new poncho, making sure that the backpack was well protected underneath. As I marched forward, the farmer who had been hidden from my view graciously turned the water off. A simple "Buenos Dias" is all that passed his lips as I shuffled by, head and body encased in an oversized blue plastic bubble. I strongly suspect that he would have liked to inquire if I were expecting nuclear fallout.

It was well past noon when I arrived back on the camino in the village of Óbanos. The grocer's deli attendant helped me select local Basque cheese and slices of paté made from wild boar's head. With red Navarran wine and a fresh baguette in hand, I once again raptured over the joys of eating in Spain.

Before returning to the camino, a walk around Óbanos revealed the imposing neo-Gothic church of St. John the Baptist. I was told that the church houses the skull of St. William in a silver reliquary box on the altar. St. William was the Duke of Aquitaine and the subject of a mystery play which has been performed here every year on the Sunday following Corpus Christi since 1965. Óbanos is famous throughout Spain for this play. The tragic story would make a great opera.

There is some question as to actual dates but on-line Spanish historians place the events in the fourteenth century. Regardless, it is fascinating and a strange tale of two saints: brother and sister, caught up in a medieval tale of rage and remorse. The church has St. William's skull in a box to prove its story.

William and his sister Felicia traveled from Aquitaine, France to make pilgrimage at Santiago de Compostela. (Presumably, they followed the same path that I took.) On the return trip, Felicia announced to her brother that she was going to give herself to God and become a hermit. She had even chosen a small town in northern Navarra for her hermitage site. William was very angry over her decision and tried to take her by force from the hermitage. Infuriated by Felicia's refusal to return to court, he killed her in a fit of rage.

Immediately consumed with grief, the contrite William set out to return to Santiago where he prayed for his soul and forgiveness. There he renounced his nobility for a life of poverty, penitence and prayer. Guilt and sadness so racked the poor man that on his way back he made it no further than Óbanos. Riddled with remorse he remained there, weeping until his death. He was buried in the Hermitage of Our Lady of Arnotegui, a short distance south of Óbanos. A sad tale it is: mortal emotions out of control, a worthy lesson for all.

A short mile and a half west on the road lay Puente La Reina. The Queen's Bridge has led pilgrims across the Arga River since the eleventh century. The bridge itself spans the Arga with six arches in a classic Romanesque design. When the river is running still, the graceful arches form full circles as they are mirrored in the crystalline water. All who come here take their cameras to the bridge, a place of tranquil beauty. No one is sure which queen made the charitable act of building the bridge but the old Basque town of Gares took the name, Queen's Bridge, with pride. Most historians credit Doña Mayor, wife of Sancho III as the queen behind the construction. Before the bridge was built, numerous ferries plied the deep river exploiting the pilgrims and travelers alike.

I checked into the Monastery of the Church of the Crucifixion run by the Padres Rapadores. Talk about sleeping in history. The building was run by the Knights Templar until the early fourteenth century. When the Templars fell, the building came under the direction of the Order of the Hospitallers of St. John and changed its name to the Iglesia Santo Cristo. During the nineteenth century Carlist wars that lasted for fifty years, it was used as a barracks while later becoming a prison and munitions arsenal. The church and monastery are now part of the Order of Padres Rapadores who originated in Germany. The monastery accommodates about one hundred pilgrims in some ten or twelve rooms.

The double bunks stood stark and clean in the great but austere building. The self-use kitchen was well outfitted and I enjoyed the long monk-style tables with benches for reading, eating and writing. The helpful staff welcomes pilgrims in the true spirit of hospitality and selfless giving. Even though this was 2012, the donation requested was only four Euros and an official Pilgrims Passport to stamp.

One of my journal entries that evening was the wish to share this joy with my grandchildren. Perhaps my legacy to them will say: go, be, live and know that the world is populated with good people full of love and joy. A hundred years from now it will not matter whether I was rich or poor, the sort of house I lived in, or the model of car I drove—but the world may be different because I shared a dream along the way.

2

KINDNESS

*We are what we think.
All that we are arises with our thoughts.
With our thoughts we make the world.*
~ Buddha

A pair of storks was preening themselves in the church bell tower as I left the monastery at daybreak. Hundreds of swallows appeared to defy the space-time continuum as their flawless swoops and turns became orchestrated whirlwinds. How is it that they never collide with the ancient stone buildings and towers? One can only imagine the gift to flow within a world of obstructions; perhaps a lesson worthy of consideration.

On this day I was introduced to pilgrimage and the Spain of myth. I watched fellow pilgrims, backs laden with more than should be, trek down a handsome wide dirt road into a medieval landscape. Until now, such places have only been in my imagination, inspired by books, art and film. We were in a gentle rolling landscape where the road meanders through vineyards, groves of olive trees and wheat fields that became a green poem to spring. There were no reminders as to what century this may be let alone what or where to purchase something we didn't need. Somehow I could feel the tension of the person I had been start to release the person I might become.

By mid-morning the sun was hot on my shoulders as I encountered the first of a few, three thousand foot high hills that lay between me and tonight's shelter. For most pilgrims, the town of Estella would be their refuge but my hip was telling me that I would sleep in a village much closer.

Though steep at times, the first hill called Eunea, rewarded the senses with fragrant honeysuckle and what we Americans know as wild tea roses. Later in the year, summer pilgrims would have the pleasure of picking wild blackberries and raspberries from the abundant vines now in bloom. Near the top I walked through the ruins of Bargota. This had been a pilgrim's hostel and monastery of the order of San Juan's Priory since 1239. A long decline began in 1440 and ended with a single hermit in 1724. I pondered the eight hundred years of history while resting on the stones that were returning to earth.

Mañeru is a story-book village that belonged to the Knights of San Juan de Jerusalem during the twelfth and thirteenth century. The old houses that lined the main street now were mostly from the sixteenth through the nineteenth century. The family crests carved into the façade of many gave historical context to the pageant played out among nobles and kings on the way to modernity. For me, a great joy of travel is to have the history of storybooks jump off the page into three dimensional realities. Mañeru is such a place. The click of my trekking poles was very alien on its weathered and worn cobblestone streets.

Mañeru lay in a sheltering dip between two hills. As I left town and began to ascend the gentle slopes of the next hill an amazing sight came into view. A beautiful medieval hilltop village rested on the crest. It is said that the Basque name of Cirauqui means, "Nest of Vipers." I didn't see any vipers but the village has had eleven hundred years to get rid of them.

The cobblestone streets are steep and wind through structures begun in the ninth century through two or three more building sprees into the fourteenth century. I climbed through the Gothic arch in the old city wall and scaled the cobblestones and steps to the very height of the village at the church of San Roman. Tile roofs were dressed in aged patinas of rusts, tans and lichen, as their canopy cascaded down the hillside; a view unchanged for over a thousand years. Further west, I could see my fellow pilgrims, picking their way down into the valley and across the Rio Salado (Salt River).

It had been a magical day, in a magical land of another place and time. I was happy but the right hip was crying out in pain like a cat that hasn't been fed. I had only walked five miles on the road but exploring the villages had added considerably more mileage. Nevertheless, I pushed on to the next village of Lorca.

I left town walking on one of the best preserved pieces of the old Roman road yet. Many segments of today's journey had been on the Roman Way but much of the rest of it has been destroyed, covered up, or repaired beyond recognition. This segment delighted me, not only for its visible history, but also because it led across the famous medieval stone bridge at Rio Salado.

Soon I was in Lorca, another quaint village where I was warmly greeted by the host, José Ramon, at the Albergue Lorca. José treated my sweaty, aching body to a chilled bowl of gazpacho and a beer on the house. I showered while waiting for my room to be prepared and a traditional Basque meal, which was to follow in José's bar.

Walking the Camino de Santiago becomes a testament to the restorative powers of the human body. Sure, the walking, climbing and exploring can sometimes stretch our physical limits but what I became cognizant of was the healing power offered by those along the way—the hospitallers, monks, nuns and volunteers who made every albergue feel like home. Shopkeepers and old men in the street who called out the familiar greeting, "Buen Camino, va con Dios," always made me feel welcome and part of their village. To them, I was not a foreigner; I belonged here.

When I arrived at the albergue, José had grabbed my backpack and carried it upstairs to my room. That act, followed with the beer and gazpacho not only said welcome, it said, "I Care." Simple acts of kindness can never be overestimated. I fear for any society that loses the grace and civility to reach out and remain human with others. The spirituality of humanity expresses itself in acts and deeds, not just with laws, legislation and words. Yes, those are necessary, but they are empty and useless unless practiced and lived from within. The wind that lifts my wings is on the thermals created by the good deeds of my fellow beings. On this day, I soared high.

José Ramon was up serving coffee and crescents as we strapped on our backpacks and dashed out into the pre-dawn countryside. I fell victim to the herd mentality that morning and found myself out the door before logic set in. My destination was only five miles down the road where a town filled with history was waiting. Estella, boasting a population of over fifteen thousand, would be the largest town on the camino since I left Pamplona.

The tranquil countryside became a continuation of the days before; oceans of wheat fields and hillsides of vineyards. Truly, this is the land of bread and wine. There were no interruptions except the village of Villatuerta, located at the midpoint of today's walk.

Estella (Spanish for star) is known to the Basque as Lizarra. The city straddles the Rio Ega, which forms a loop through the western part of the old town. Estella was established in 1090 by King Sancho Ramirez. He built it to attract settlement of the wealthier French who were streaming through on their pilgrimage to Santiago. He visualized the town as a commercial center which would bolster the location as a trade route for merchants and serve as an extended rest stop for pilgrims. The stage was set for an influx of artists, stonemasons and builders who came and created the cathedrals, palaces, bridges and hospitals that continue to amaze us today.

Estella was briefly a Camelot, a city where knights plied the roadways and wise kings ruled the land. Numerous wars have destroyed most of the protective castles and city walls, leaving only the bones and ruins to tell us its legend. Still, the town is a museum and a testament to medieval times. Its story, like a book, remains open and ready to read.

I arrived at ten thirty and set about immediately to explore the Palace of the Kings of Navarra, now a museum and art gallery. This handsome Romanesque edifice was built by King Sancho el Sabio in the late twelfth century. The pilgrim's guide said that Sancho used the Benedictine center of Cluny in France as his model. I left the palace through a side plaza, and stepped on to a wide bridge spanning the river.

The Ega was running clear with trout hovering in the fast moving shallows. On the right side, a few young men were fishing from the banks. The river formed a U shaped loop to the left of the bridge where it encircled a very large well-maintained green space known as the Parque de los Llanos. There were two medieval stone convents located within its grounds.

The Convento Antiguo de San Benito el Real is now abandoned. Its pastiche of Renaissance and Baroque architecture give silent testimony to a grander history, when her elegant façade had few peers. Across the park, beyond hedge row and trees was the Franciscan Convent of Santa Clara. The nuns have had a convent on the river flats since the thirteenth century but these buildings are credited to the fifteenth or even seventeenth century. It remains a cloistered convent.

I dozed along the tree-lined river path on a park bench, dreaming of life in this beautiful city and the impermanence of empires. The river soothed and splashed in the background as she sang of her journey and of the mysteries along her shores.

I checked into the Hospital de Peregrinas on Calle de la Rua when it opened at one p.m. The remodeled old two story building can accommodate one hundred four pilgrims in four rooms with an overflow dormitory when needed. The welcoming and friendly staff took me on a tour of the facilities which included a modern kitchen, large dining area, laundry and patio out back. After a hot shower, a call home to my daughter and catch-up on e-mails, I was ready for Jamon Serrano (Spanish dry cured ham) with a sampler of local cheese, crusty bread and red wine.

Across the plaza from the Palace of the Kings of Navarra begins a flight of stone stairs, which are perhaps twenty feet wide, ascending the hillside to the twelfth century Church of San Pedro de la Rua. It was in this imposing, fortified setting that the Kings of Navarra took their oath. War has taken its toll on the beautiful cloister; the greater of two sides now missing. The walls around the courtyard were stacked with corbels, carvings and broken columns, evidently the victims from both interior and exterior clashes. The beautiful interior of the church was staged as a museum with appropriate lighting and guided tours available.

Despite the throngs of tourists and pilgrims who stream through, the church continues to hold mass daily.

Like most Spanish cities, in the late evening the residents of Estella pour into the streets and cafes for a communal social hour. The daily promenade of old and young alike brings lovers onto benches, little children into play and couples slowly strolling arm-in-arm.

I walked to the central plaza where dozens of cafés came alive as friends and families assembled to celebrate another day in their life. All around the perimeter servers had set up tables under umbrellas with crisp napery and polished glassware. The camaraderie of the community was infectious as they shared food, told stories, drank wine and, with great restraint, watched their children become drenched as they splashed in the fountain. I joined the celebration with wine and dinner at a café overlooking the festive scene. My appetizer of romaine greens and fresh white anchovies was dressed in olive oil and lemon juice. The entrée of grilled lamb chops and a side of roasted red peppers stuffed with bacalao (salt cod) was Basque cuisine at its best.

The next day I walked into Navarran wine country and the first village on the road out of Estella wanted to get that point across. Irache wine producers have installed a "wine fountain" directly into the wall along the pathway. Since most pilgrims carry the scallop shell, their badge of identity became a drinking vessel. The excellent red wine flows for all who turn the spigot. There is no supervision or attendant nearby—just a pleasant show of hospitality and crafty marketing. Vineyards were on either side of the road; they climb up the hillsides and completely surround the ancient Monastery of Irache, which was further down the path. The abbey was Benedictine from Visigoth times but they had to vacate in 1985 due to the lack of novitiates.

My right hip had developed a steady pain that came on earlier every day. Sometimes that leg seemed to just disappear from underneath me; one minute there would be two legs, the next moment only one. At times like this the trekking poles became more than just an aid. I had started listening to my inner voice and noticed that when I allowed the suffering and pain to dominate my thoughts, the voice became weaker as the pain increased. I felt certain that what I needed to learn was to release pain and suffering. I was anxious to learn that lesson.

As I rested over coffee and pastry at the quaint bar and bakery in the village of Azqueta, I contemplated the message of suffering. I wrote in my journal, "I am determined to go beyond these obstacles of pain. I will not accept suffering, I will yield to the lesson and I am going to walk to Santiago."

Knowing a truth doesn't make it so; first one must accept it as personal truth. I had been a practitioner of Vippassana meditation for several years and understood the teachings and practice, yet here I was searching for an answer that I should have learned long ago. "Perhaps there's more forgiveness to learn," I thought and limped on down the road.

The village of Villamayor de Monjardin was only another mile along the camino and I conceded that I would rest and spend the night there. For today's entire walk I could see the ruins of the Castle of St. Stephen crowning the peak of Monjardin. After Azqueta, the road began a steady climb in the hot sun to reach its village.

That was the hottest day on the entire pilgrimage. My thermometer registered in the low nineties and there were no trees for refuge. Miles of vineyards marched across the gentle landscape as far as the eye could see. In the middle of the expanse stood the strange troll-like, cone shaped mountain of Monjardin. The hot treeless village was stuck in its side and an old crumbling castle sat on top like a hat.

Two albergue were listed in my guidebook for the town but when I arrived there was only one. The other had been forced to close. My option was to walk another five miles or stay at The Hogar Monjardin which was run by a Dutch ecumenical group.

The building was a converted village house with twenty beds in four rooms on the second floor and attic. I was shown to the attic which I shared with two French women. Thick stone walls kept the heat out and the afternoon vanished into night as I fell into a deep sleep.

3

THE BORGIA LEGACY

Remind yourself daily that there is no way to happiness;
Rather, happiness is the way.
~Wayne W. Dyer

The long rest in Villamayor was helpful. I walked eleven miles today with minimal discomfort through vineyards and villages that have served the area since Roman times. The road was a mirror of yesterday's walk until it started a gradual climb to the village of Sansol. I passed a few Baroque palaces perched on steep cobblestone streets before arriving at the eighteenth century Church of San Zoilo from which Sansol derived its name. From this vantage point I could see that the village sat upon a high bluff which dropped down rather steeply into a ravine where the Linares River flowed. On the western side of the river sat my destination, Torres del Rio.

Torres del Rio (tower of the river) is an enigma. It sits in the gulley of the Linares with no possibility of mounting a defense, a prime deciding factor for building all medieval villages. It is known to have existed before the Muslim occupation and yet it survived, to be recaptured by the Christians in 914. Here in one of the most charming villages to date, the namesake tower was built by the Knights Templar. Excited to explore the town, I scrambled down the steep and narrow dirt path from Sansol into the ravine and across the bridge.

The town may be built in a gulley but it is not flat. The terrain rises up from the river in bumps and terraces that become a small mountain. It was constructed—as is, where is, on the hillside. After eleven miles on the road, I huffed and puffed my way up to the central plaza and the old three story stone pilgrim's hostel, Casa Mariela. After a quick shower and lunch, I set out to discover the quixotic Iglesia Del Santo Sepulcro. Mario, at the front desk, said that it was behind Casa Mariela. "It is just out the door and to your right, señor."

There, resplendent in golden stone, stood an octagonal three story structure crowned with a tower—the Torre del Rio. Clearly this was a work created by the same craftsmen as Eunate, but this church was double the height, had a tower and no exterior cloister. I ran to the entrance but found the door padlocked. There was no posting as to hours, so I returned to my new information source. "It's after four p.m. and the caretaker should be there—I'll call her," Mario said. His voice moved from courteous to inquisitive to silent, then, "entonces quando . . . . hasta cinco? Turning to me with an exasperated look, "She will be there at five," he said.

At 4:50 I joined a small group of five or six pilgrims who were also waiting to see the interior of the Holy Sepulcher. At 5:10 a middle aged, robust woman wearing a skirt, blouse and red sweater came down the hill and joined our group. She began rummaging through a well-worn purse and seemed quite surprised to find a key with an old paper tag attached. Without a word to anyone she unlocked the door, switched on the lights and sat down behind a makeshift desk. "Three Euros," she announced to the group, "if you want to see our beautiful church."

It turned out that the señora was a wealth of helpful information. She appeared to have a great affection for the old building and the stories that it had to tell. The dates of construction were not known but there were records of a monastery being attached to the church in the twelfth century. It belonged to the Military Order of the Knights of the Holy Sepulcher in Jerusalem, which later became known as the Knights Templar.

Stone benches had been built into six of the eight walls, with an altar niche becoming the focus on another wall in a pleasing symmetrical well-proportioned room. The niche looked very much like the mihrab in a mosque, giving further evidence to accounts that the Templars used Moorish craftsmen. Directly opposing the altar niche was a mirror version of the arch containing the annex and a stone circular staircase which ascended to the tower.

The tower appears to have been a beacon where fire could be lit at night to guide wayward Christians to sanctuary—but that is pure conjecture. The building cannot be seen until one looks down upon it from the bluff. The original function of this encrypted masterpiece is another mystery. Some historians have suggested that it was a funeral chapel. That presumption is based on recent excavations that have found several tombs. To the lay observer, the small octagonal shape could not support a large ceremony as we may imagine in today's churches.

The stone-work throughout is breathtaking. It is, in the simplest of terms, an eight-sided cylinder rising three open levels to the crossed arches and Islamic-inspired cupola. The eaves are supported with corbels carved into a variety of vegetable and animal designs. The señora explained that the theme of the capitals was of Christ's death and resurrection. She allowed me to read from the pages of a Spanish language information guide that provided additional amazing data: Divine geometry seems to have guided the master plan; designing the width of the dome to be precisely the height of the walls. The height to the first floor capitals is precisely the height of the dome and other details confirm that the Holy Sepulcher in Jerusalem was the model. As we prepared to leave, our guide said, "Wait, you need to come to the center and speak." Every word spoken, even softly, seemed to hover in the room with a resonance that could very well be the voice of God.

The window of my second floor room opened to look over the plaza, down to the river and out to the valley in the west. As dusk settled in, I placed my arms across the sill and daydreamed while watching a pair of stork practice landing and take-off from a nearby bell tower. Swallows were circling the plaza in such frenzy that they were reduced to a blur.

Dark clouds had been assembling on the western horizon, and suddenly without warning they shot daggers of gold light into the plains beyond. A rumble of thunder soon followed and the storm headed my way. The swallows were flying so close to the buildings that I withdrew my arms to avoid a collision. A bird in the hand was not what I had in mind.

The storm rolled into town with more beauty and majesty than any I had ever seen. It was a light and sound show projected from a big grey and purple flying carpet of clouds. The rain bounced off the cobblestones and formed into rivulets and streams that ran down the hill to join the Rio Linares.

That night I dreamed. I saw my body, white as marble—suspended, lying horizontal mid-air. The setting was in a garden so lush that in my wildest fantasy I could not have imagined it. Clear luminous water was being poured over me from a source out of frame. The floating alabaster body was youthful, hairless and held a smile of pleasure as the glowing water passed over it. I watched from my dream and yet experienced the event as though I were both the observer and the observed. The sensation seemed so real that I assumed the body was me, being reborn and christened as an adult. I awoke confused, fully expecting to be naked and wet. The gentle rain falling just beyond my open window morphed from the dream and back again—each one confirming the other. I returned to the pillow, joyous and happy to be cleansed and confirmed. I wanted to return to dreamland. "Every morning we are born again. What we do today is what matters most." ~Buddha

The rain spent the night soothing my dreams and cooling the air before heading east at daybreak. The fresh cooler air added lift to my step as I climbed the mountain and waved farewell to the magic and mysteries of Torres del Rio. From the top of Mount Poyo I could see Viana, and beyond to the industrial spread of Logroño—eleven miles on the western horizon. There were the makings of new storms hovering over the west and northern plains. During the trek across open farmland several storm cells crossed the camino and performed threatening dances to the south and north. None of them rained on me.

Viana's history would fill a library but the big story is its connection to the infamous Borgia family. The Borgia of Spain, like the Medici of Florence, was a rich politically motivated family whose corrupt ambitions led Rodrigo Borgia to become Pope Alexander VI. Pope Alexander had four bastard children whom he publicly recognized during his reign. Two of them obtained their own infamy: Lucretia and Cesár. Pope Alexander groomed Cesár for church leadership, giving him the position of Bishop of Pamplona at age fifteen and that of cardinal when he was eighteen. The arrogant Spanish boy was a ruthless terror to the family's many enemies. In Italy, Cesár was hated and feared. He quickly became known for rape, incest, robbery and murder, while the Pope continued to provide him new toys of stolen power and status.

The story of the Borgia family is a good read but here I will only give a thumbnail synopsis of Cesár's return and death in Spain: At the time of Pope Alexander's death in 1503, Cesár was commanding the Papal armies. The new Pope, Pius III, continued to support Cesár's position and holdings but within twenty-six days in office, the Pope was dead. Cesár's dominoes began to fall quickly as Cardinal Giuliano Della Rovere became Pope Julius II. This Pope, who hated the Borgia family, seized Cesár's vast holdings and titles in Italy and exiled him to Spain in 1504.

Fate struck again. While fighting in Spain with questionable loyalty, Borgia was captured and thrown in prison at the Castle La Mota near Valladolid. He is rumored to have escaped the fortress on a rope, resulting in a fall which caused him serious injury.

This was a time of great turmoil in Spain. Queen Isabel had died leaving the throne to several hopefuls: There was King Ferdinand who would rule through their daughter Juana la Loca and Juana's son, the Hapsburg prince Carlos V. In addition, there was a contingent of French and Italians who were armed to take a slice of the Spanish pie. Battles raged as all contenders plotted to take the spoils. In 1507 the rich city of Viana came under threat from the French and elected General Borgia to lead the defense against the invasion led by Count Louie de Beaumont.

It is said that he showed great bravery as he defended the city and its castle under siege. He died on the battlefield, where he had ridden out alone to die with honor. Viana laid Cesár to rest in its cathedral, the thirteenth century Iglesia de Santa Maria de la Asuncion. His marble tomb was beneath the altar with an inscription that read, "Here lays a little earth, one who was feared by all, who held peace and war in his hands."

All in Christendom were not pleased. A few years later, the bishop had Borgia's body moved outside the church to unconsecrated ground under the entrance walkway, to be exact. Cesár Borgia—Prince of the church, a friend and model for Leonardo de Vinci and subject for Niccolo Machiavelli's allegory, The Prince—was condemned to lay underfoot the populace.

I too walked on Borgia's marble slab on my way into the cathedral. I joined a few pilgrims to attend Sunday mass at the Church of Santa Maria and found his tomb directly in our path. The name Cesár Borgia and relative dates were clearly engraved in the walkway stone. However, there are numerous online accounts that the Archbishop of Pamplona has ordered his remains to be reinstated within the church proper via an edict of 2007. Poor Cesár, there was to be no rest for him, even in death.

Viana's Albergue Andres Munoz is located in a converted monastery adjacent to the ruins of the Iglesia San Pedro. The two buildings are in a park-like setting which overlooks the city of Logroño to the west. The albergues conversion is a masterpiece combining modern comfort in an ancient building. The charm continues into a large dining hall and terrace overlooking the camino and long expanse of valley below.

The half-standing Gothic walls of the old church provide wonderful details illustrating the construction techniques of the period. What I saw from the street was the façade wall and gate, framed with a triumphal arch and lovely Gothic plaques, columns and figures. It came as a surprise when I stepped inside on a grass field and discovered the missing side walls and roof. During the Carlist Wars in 1833, the church had been used as a barracks and it took serious cannon shot leading to the collapse some ten years later.

Viana is history that I could step into. The streets are peopled with families, merchants and vendors who express their happiness at the cafés, bars, and church. After Sunday mass, a band began to play in the cobblestone church square. Some children, mostly girls, formed an impromptu dance while little boys played at make believe bull fights.

Horns and handlebars outfitted over a bike wheel became the bull that chased would-be toreros around the plaza. The adults strolled, laughed and celebrated life over plates of tapas, wine and sangrias. Grandparents sat with canes and walkers, proudly pointing out their gene-bearers, frolicking in the sunny plaza.

4

A WOMAN ALONE

Perhaps 5,000 generations of humans have walked the surface of the earth since we first emerged in Africa about 100,000 years ago, and of them, the ones living in this century will ultimately determine our fate.
~ Michio Kaku

Few towns on the camino (or Northern Spain, for that matter) have the urban sprawl of Logroño. This city of perhaps 150,000 souls has paved its way across the eastern border of La Rioja with little respect for an illustrious history. My legs and hip ached as I trekked on its hot treeless carpet of concrete into the city center.

Dominating the geographic corner between Aragon, Navarra and Castile/Leon, Logroño's unique position on the Rio Ebro became its greatness and its downfall. Rulers from each of the surrounding king states took turn courting the city and destroying it. The town has suffered more wars than perhaps any other Spanish city. From the twelfth through the twentieth century, Logroño suffered no less than thirteen wars which have destroyed the medieval charm of its famed monuments, castles, walls and pilgrim hospices.

Today, Logroño is a thriving university town that is the capital of La Rioja, one of the most important wine districts in all Spain. The historic plaza mercado is dominated by the fourteenth century Cathedral de Santa Maria de la Redonda. Cafés and tapa bars spread out with colorful umbrellas across the plaza and down the side streets. Despite its losses, the old town has charm and the patina that only time and wear can give to cobblestones and sun drenched architecture.

I decided to walk another seven miles and spend the night at Navarette. At the western edge of the old city I noticed that something was different in the way that I walked. It was on a steep cobblestone street that the dawn of truth hit. I had left my trekking poles at a café on the plaza. Fortunately, the server had taken them inside where I found them waiting for me behind the bar.

The exit west continued through modern commercial Logroño where banks, beauty salons and wine tasting bodegas lined the way. The stark contrast of modern sprawl to the old city's medieval past came as a shock to many of us pilgrims on the historical path. Unlike previous towns, here the camino scallop shell markers were few and far between with little indication when pilgrims were supposed to change streets. I had to inquire three times when the absence of markers made street choices difficult. I knew to go west but here there were several choices going in that direction. It is amazing how much longer it takes to walk on a mile of concrete, along commercial strip-malls than on a mile of shady path in the forest, with birdsong and waterfalls.

Navarette has retained the charm of its medieval heritage. Family crests and shields are carved into the facades of stone and brick buildings clearly identifying the town's noble heritage. Home tonight is the official Albergue de Peregrinos located in a handsome two story brick building with arched arcade. After a three p.m. lunch, I took refuge from the heat in the sixteenth century Church of the Assumption. Navarette is on a hillside and the church holds an imposing position overlooking the town and vineyards beyond. The day's walk had been long and difficult and I wanted to let go and be in the joy of the moment. I sat in the cool interior to meditate and reflect on the magic and wonder of my journey; I was walking the sacred way of history and myth.

I began preparing for my pilgrimage by reading the story of Saint James and the city of his namesake, Santiago de Compostela. I ordered three of the most popular guidebooks and several tomes covering the history of the Moors, Charlemagne and the Knights Templar during the crusades. The more that I read, the sooner I wanted to be here walking in those footsteps. And equally interesting to me, the camino passes through three great cultures of diversity in food, language and customs. It begins in Basque country, continues through Old Castile and Leon and climbs into the mythical mountainous Celtic region known as Galicia.

The pilgrimage to Santiago hit its zenith from the eleventh through the fourteenth centuries. Early Christians were committed to pilgrimage at least once in their lives. There were three locations they could go: Jerusalem, Rome or Santiago de Compostela. After Jerusalem fell to the Moors, Santiago became the pilgrimage of choice. Traditionally, when they walked out the front door of their homes they were on pilgrimage. Unlike today, there were no buses, trains and planes to take them to a starting point. Christians from the British Isles, Scandinavia and all of Europe found their way across the continent to be united at the beginning in the French Pyrenees, or somewhere along the Camino Francés. From there, they entered the pass west which has funneled humanity to the Atlantic coast for over one hundred thousand years. Once in Spain, large portions of the old Roman road were serviceable as some sections are today.

The great Way of Saint James continues to be walked by people of every faith, every culture and from most countries. Many are Christians who today, as in medieval times walk to strengthen their faith and relationship with God. Some come for their health, others for the physical challenges. And many are at a crossroads in life (like me), looking for time alone on the pilgrimage to help sort things out. On any one night in a pilgrim's albergue, as many as twenty countries can be represented. English and Spanish are the two official languages which includes signage in cathedrals, museums and most shops. I never witnessed any discrimination as to age, sex, nationality, skin color or religion. No one was ever questioned as to his or her faith or requested to participate in a religious service. The Camino de Santiago offers acceptance and shelter to all—few places on earth can make such a claim.

I awoke the next morning with a full blown cold. I possessed every possible misery that can be attributed to the affliction. The inventory included headache, sinus congestion, cough, sore throat and a runny nose. I was miserable. I decided to walk anyway with the medicine of sunshine and the lush Rioja vineyards to brighten the way.

On the way out of town I joined a group of fellow pilgrims at a street-side bar for morning coffee. New comers are always asked where they plan to stop for the night and of course "where did you start?" Since my destination was just four miles up the road, a couple from Santa Fe inquired why such a short walk. "You have a cold, do you have any medication to take for it?" they asked. I said that I did not have any relief until we came to a town large enough to have a pharmacy. They came to my rescue with cold meds taken from a well outfitted arsenal of emergency supplies.

The camino quickly becomes a family of compassionate caregivers who look after each other with sincere concern and friendship. Pilgrims greet each other as friends, not strangers. By the time they reach Santiago de Compostela they have been both receiver and giver many times over. The camaraderie becomes a powerful healing aspect of pilgrimage.

Ventosa is a picture perfect medieval town worthy of a Spanish travel poster. The village of one hundred fifty souls, two dogs and a cat sits on a rise a slight distance to the south of the camino proper. The Albergue San Saturnino welcomed me early so I could take to bath and bed for a restorative break. The San Saturnino is located in a medieval stone hostel which has been restored with charm and a reserved artistic touch. I was thankful to be there. That day, I gave in to the camino, to my body and to this delightful village. I surrendered to the healing.

The next day I was better, much better in fact. The early dawn shed enough light to pick my way through the village and onto a dirt path that returned to the camino. The landscape was a continuation of Rioja's fame—vineyards. I soon caught up with a woman who walked slower than I did—which was a first. Martha was from Nebraska. She was a teacher, mother, average middle class American who was on her first trip out of the United States. She had read about the Camino and dreamed about seeing herself walking across a foreign landscape—a landscape where much of the history she taught took place.

We walked together for some three hours while she shared the fears that she had of being "a woman alone" in a strange land. Before leaving she suffered from anxiety about what to wear, what to take and what to do for protection. After all, "most of the camino would be through rural countryside where savage dogs and perhaps snakes would be encountered." She marveled at her own strength of will to overcome the imagined obstacles and to take the pilgrimage.

The simple act of walking the ancient path had restored her faith in self and released her from fear of the unknown. She was overjoyed with discovering new towns, new sites of great historical events and, most of all, sharing her new magic with fellow pilgrims.

"My life has always been so ordinary, doing what others expected of me. I went to school, to college, got married, raised a family and taught school. As I turned middle age, I began to question. Is that all there is? What reason did I have to question a good husband, successful children and a comfortable home that was paid for? It's just that I didn't feel alive," Martha said.

She had been surprised, when her husband and children encouraged her to take a month away and follow her dream of walking the camino. She confessed that she almost hadn't come because the family's encouragement made it seem like she wasn't needed anymore. All of the old fears were whispering the dangers and reasons not to go on a wild goose chase. Martha was astute at observing and becoming responsible for her own feelings.

"I have become alive and awakened to who I am for the first time. I have so much more strength and wisdom to take home to my family. I can't wait to tell them how much I love them."

She left me in Najera where I was to spend a magical day learning the amazing story of a king and his falcon.

If for no other reason, the Camino de Santiago should be walked to discover some of the most interesting towns in the world. Each of the villages and towns that I entered seemed more special than the one before. That was true of Najera, a real jewel on the pilgrim's path, a town of some 8,500 that most of us have never heard of.

Najera has many buildings, churches, monuments and mythical stories that both amaze and amuse visitors. It was the capitol of the kingdom of Navarre in the eleventh and twelfth century. Today you can tour the magnificent tombs of the kings, queens and knights from that period in the Royal Pantheon. The Pantheon and cloisters are part of the Monastery of Santa Maria whose construction was triggered by King Garcia III. He made a miraculous discovery while hunting in 1044. The King's falcon chased a white dove into the red sandstone caves common to this area. He followed the bird. A light was streaming from deep within the cave—there in ethereal glow sat an old wooden statue of the Virgin Mary and a vase of fresh white lilies. To Garcia, who had been fighting the march of Islam across Spain, this was a sign from God and reinforcement to his Christian faith.

A chapel was ordered to be built at the very mouth of the cave. The chapel was soon followed with a church and monastery which were consecrated in 1052. Very little remains of the original because a much grander replacement was built in the sixteenth century. Pope Alexander (The Borgia Pope) made the monastery an independent abbacy which led to the reconstruction that pilgrims now visit.

The elaborate cloister is known as the Claustro de los Caballeros (Cloister of the Knights) because so many are buried there. The ornate sarcophagi are rich in detail with a full size stone likeness of each knight lying on top, dressed in full armor with sword in hand. I was impressed that one knight had his faithful hound curled up at his feet. Sides of many of the sarcophagus were carved with the deeds and tributes achieved by the knight within. The arches of the stone cloister are considered among the finest in Spain, each one unique with delicate filigree carvings.

The man that united the warring Christian knights into a Holy War was Pope Urban II in 1095. The Muslim hordes had committed heinous atrocities against the Christians throughout the Holy Land, who were demanding that the Pope provide support and troops. Urban went on tour to plead with all the Royal courts to give money and knights to avenge their lands and birthright. Through the church's leadership the first in a series of nine Crusades was launched that would last for over one hundred years.

The Royal Pantheon has thirty tombs rendered in an ornate solemn manner that is further dignified with subdued lighting that highlights the figures and carvings to dramatic effect. Impressive for me was the tomb of Queen Doña Blanca de Castile y Navarre from 1156. The queen and her clothing appear to have been turned to stone by some magic spell. She is the quintessential beauty in cold stone, life frozen in death at full bloom.

I passed through the cloister to the tombs of the kings and further behind was another passageway. I entered a cave—its walls red with stone and earth. There in the deepest part was a statue of the virgin with a vase of fresh lilies at her feet. I almost expected to see a falcon nearby, dove in talon.

I may have spent the day with nobility but I spent that night in what can best be remembered as an authentic medieval pilgrimage experience. The large single story hostel was described in my guide book as "somewhat cramped." That was the biggest understatement since King Garcia entered the cave and said, "Ah, fresh lilies."

I knew something was amiss since the long queue of pilgrims was kept outside and allowed into the plain military-style "induction center" single file. Each pilgrim's data was entered into the official log book by a somber gentleman seated behind a long grey table. Standing to his left in front of barrack style doors was a woman who had a mission. She spoke loudly and with the authority that only practice can give. She was holding a bed assignment chart and pencil.

It was always the same tone and command when a pilgrim finished registering, "Where is your mochila (backpack)? Put your shoes and poles on the rack and follow me." We entered through the double doors into one large hot room outfitted with one hundred double bunks. This was a test to compromise anyone who might have a sense of privacy. The bunks were pushed together so that four rows touched each other from side to side. There were two narrow aisles. That meant that the two rows of bunks down the middle not only touched from side to side but end to end. Everyone in a side row would be sleeping with twenty-five and those down the double center would essentially be in one bed with fifty folks. Did I mention that this was a co-ed experience?

I was ready to go back and sleep with the kings in the crypts of the Royal Pantheon. The señora would carefully study the chart and assign a bunk which resulted in strange sleeping partners. She would slap a bunk, make a mark on her chart and announce, "This is your bed, number twenty-seven, do not trade with anyone else, I know where you are." To make matters more complicated than they already were, she did not take the bunks sequentially down a row. Surely some devilish and medieval codebook had taken over our lives.

My bunk was one of those in the middle tier. That night I waited to enter the oven of bodies until the last minute possible. The lights were out and the señora was patrolling the aisles assuring compliance with her rules, "No mingling and silence please." As I slid under the sheet my feet jammed into something strange near the foot of the bed. It seemed somewhat familiar and organic—maybe at one time it had been alive. I let out a muffled cry of alarm as I sat up too quickly to avoid the low overhead bunk. By then, our overseer was by my side and I whispered concerns about the strange thing in my bed. "Ah" she said after a brief inspection "it's just the feet of the very tall man on the other end. Why don't you let him sleep? His feet won't bother you."

5

HANGING THE INNOCENT

Talking about a path is not walking that path.
Thinking about life is not living it.
Lao Tzu ~ *Tao Te Ching*

Wide earthen paths wound through rolling countryside for most of today's twelve mile walk to Santo Domingo de Calzada. At one point the road led up a 2500 foot mountain to a village perched on top.

Pilgrims on the camino enjoy one of the longest and most pristine hikes in the world. Devoid of billboards or modern buildings strung along the roadside, the path leads from one historic medieval village to the next. Every day we pass oceans of wheat, miles of rolling vineyards and sweet smelling orchards of almonds, olives and fruit trees. Shepherds herd flocks of fleecy sheep that flow like liquid down hillsides, across the pilgrim's pathways and on to greener pastures. There is a timeless thread of tradition on the camino that reassures "all is well with the world." Occasionally we would come upon a stark twenty-first century reminder that other realities still exist. Cirueña was one of those surprises.

Like many countries around the world Spain has fallen victim to overbuilding and speculation on the potential for growth. During the first five years of this century towns like Cirueña built modern suburbs of condos and apartments that are packed together like beehives with wire fences and huge metal gates. I entered street after street with thousands of these inhuman warrens on the eastern approach to the old village. It was eerily empty. The same was true of the golf course, the club house and the bar. All buildings had a simple sign on the gate or fence: Se Vende (for sale). For me, the setting was apocalyptic. On the positive side, there are no other examples such as Cirueña elsewhere on the camino.

Five miles further I came to Santo Domingo de la Calzada, a town inhabited with stories, history and myth. The Abadia Cistercian Convent was to be my home that night. The kind and hospitable nuns house thirty-four souls (men and women) in six rooms. Here I was able to do laundry and snooze in the garden.

I reflected on America's two longest hiking trails that have no sanctuary along the way to rest weary bones and bruised feet. The Appalachian Trail and The Pacific Crest Trail take hikers through the most beautiful and finest wilderness and parkland the country has to offer. However, trekkers must take tent, food supplies and all gear necessary to survive for days and sometimes weeks without support or supply. To do this, each hiker must carry a forty to fifty pound backpack. I would love to walk both great trails but cannot carry the weight. For that reason, the camino is a gift that keeps on giving through the kindness and generosity of many organizations, countries, individuals and, like tonight, Cistercian Nuns.

The real life journey of Domingo Garcia to that of Saint Dominic de la Calzada is one of many inspirational stories of selfless service to pilgrims on the way to Santiago. Born to peasant parents in 1019, the young shepherd boy dreamed of becoming a priest in the service to God. Domingo began studies in the Benedictine monastery but performed so poorly that he was rejected as a priest.

Rejected by the church but resolute in his convictions, Domingo, at the age of fifteen, became a hermit in the forests that bordered the Oja River. He was inspired in a dream to join the service of the Bishop San

Gregorio who came to improve the lives of those in the Rioja region. They cleared wilderness, built roads and bridges for several years until Gregorio's death. Domingo had seen what roads and bridges could do to improve the plight of pilgrims on the Camino—a calling he gladly answered. He was inspired to return to the Oja valley where he spent the remainder of his life in service to travelers on the Way of Saint James.

He cleared forests, built a stone bridge over the river and constructed thirty-seven kilometers of roadway between Najera and Redecilla del Camino. King Garcia III gave him permission to turn an old fort into a pilgrim hospice which soon evolved into a village. Future kings liked having better roads and bridges in their realm so they continued to support Domingo's improvements with monies and labor. He spent the final decade of his life devoted to erecting the church where he would be buried.

There are two miracles attributed to Santo Domingo. The first one occurred early during his career when a village gave him as many trees as he could cut in one day. The miracle: He only cut one tree. A band of angels appeared and cut all the trees necessary by sundown.

The larger miracle surrounding Santo Domingo seems hinged to a myth that occurs in many European communities. It is called the "hanged innocent." Our story is about a German family: father, mother and son. On their pilgrimage to Santiago, they stay overnight in the local inn at Santo Domingo de la Calzada. The innkeeper's daughter takes a fancy to the handsome lad and propositions him. The boy, on pilgrimage with his parents, rejected her. Enraged by his rejection, the girl has a silver cup hidden in his luggage which she reported as missing. Soon, authorities "discovered" the vessel, arrested the young man and, as was the custom, hanged the thief.

The distraught parents continued their pilgrimage to Santiago de Compostela. On their return to Germany they once again stayed in Santo Domingo. The sadness of loss that remained heavy on their hearts became an inspiration to visit the tree where the boy died. Much to the couples delight he greeted them with enthusiasm while still hanging from the gibbet. He explained to the joyous parents that Santo Domingo supported him throughout the ordeal and that he was well and healthy. The parents dash off to tell the city official that "their son is alive, come cut him down."

The official was just sitting down to dinner when the happy couple burst in with their good news. On the table were two handsome roast chickens, ready for the carving. Upon hearing the story, the official picked up his carving knife and said, "That boy is no more alive than these two roasted chickens." The chickens immediately jump up, become whole with feathers and all and fly out the window, cackling loudly as they go.

The "chicken story" remains a miracle to many and a myth to the rest of us. Regardless, the cathedral has reinforcements: High above the Tomb of Santo Domingo is a gilded cage containing two white live chickens. It is claimed that they are direct descendants of the original two "roasted chickens." I am certain that the two cackling chickens living high in holy splendor while I was there were alive. Standing below, the aroma drifting down confirmed its organic origin. According to church officials, a piece of the branch that the boy hung from is displayed high in the transept over Santo Domingo's tomb.

Like Santo Domingo, there are many modern "volunteer saints" who work hard to insure that the camino path and facilities remain in the best condition possible. The twenty-first century has seen a real renaissance on the camino with over 250,000 pilgrims walking or cycling it annually. In the early 1990s the count was as low as ten thousand but it has continued a steady climb when it reached 180,000 in the holy year of 2004. The annual increase in 2012 is close to twenty percent.

Villages along the way are invigorated to meet the challenges to better serve modern pilgrims. More historic buildings are being converted into charming hostels with modern kitchens, laundries and internet as standard service. Good home cooked meals can be found in every village at very reasonable prices and usually includes wine. Spain remains a meat and potatoes cuisine but gradually vegetarian fare has started appearing in a few cities. Books with popular authors such as Shirley MacLaine and Paulo Coelho have been helpful by telling their personal Camino stories. In 2010 the film, *The Way,* with Martin Sheen and Emilio Estevez (who wrote and directed it) was premiered in

Santiago. A year later the film's wide distribution in the Americas and Europe gave millions a visual story that became a personal invitation to walk the camino.

Today I will be saying good-by to La Rioja and enter Castile and Leon, the largest autonomous region in Spain. The region is so large that over fifty percent of the Camino Francés passes through just three of its southern provinces, Burgos, Palencia and Leon. Granon is the last village in La Rioja; here grapes are gone, replaced with irrigated tracts of potatoes and vast fields of poppies. I made my silent farewell over coffee in this quaint Jacobean village. Soon I would be in the land of castles and El Cid.

Compared to my fellow pilgrims I appeared to be on a countryside walk. Perhaps they thought that I was a birder or maybe someone out to catch butterflies without a net—crazy old Don Quixote wandering the plains without a horse or Sancho Panza.

Many were headed for Belorado in nine miles, VillaFranca Montes De Oca in sixteen miles, or even beyond. I was meandering down the road for a short walk to Redecilla Del Camino. The ever present pilgrims on bicycles were in larger numbers than usual—some in groups of seven or eight. Today's wide dirt track provided enough room for walkers and cyclists to pass without interruption but there have been times requiring more caution.

Often the wide tracks would narrow to single person, two foot wide paths, with thick foliage on either side. I would be absorbed in the landscape, perhaps listening to a bird song and not be aware of an approaching bike. Many times they would remain silent, close on my heels and just wait to be discovered. That is not the best approach to pass a grumpy old man—or anyone else for that matter. When startled by bikers on the creep I had to suppress two conflicting urges—either let anger rule or jump into the weeds. "Bikes have bells, use them," I would call out. Sometimes I would add, "Don't you know old men are hard of hearing?" I graciously thanked all who used their bells or announced themselves. One man solved the problem by saying, "Beep, beep." "I like your bell" I said.

The path came to a rise where several pilgrims, both walkers and bikers, had gathered in front of two large billboards. The very size required viewers to appear awestruck as they stared at the monoliths. This modern garish welcome was a first on the camino. Leon and Castile wanted all to know of the greatness, history and importance we were about to enter. Here on the path it was overkill. What got our attention as helpful was a much smaller overview map of the camino as it passed through the region.

A wide vista of countryside to the west ends in an elevated haze on the far horizon—the foreshadowing of mountains to come. Redecilla Del Camino is a very small village of 150 but it has been serving pilgrims on the camino since the eleventh century. A welcome gift from Leon and Castile that I received with thanks was the weather. It had been sunny but chilly all day—as I arrived in the village the temperature barely reached sixty degrees.

The town may be small but my home for the night was in the medieval Hospital de San Lazaro which has been converted to the Albergue San Lazaro and bar. The old building is comfortable with ten beds in each of four rooms. Most of the occupants that night were a college age crowd with a fun group of Irish finding humor in their own bruises, blisters and torn tendons.

Every hiker on the camino will tell you that they had prepared for the trip. I heard stories nightly about forays to REI, reading camino guides and the time they took to choose backpacks and shoes. So why were so many becoming crippled or injured in the feet and legs? Most common problem: they did not take warnings and advice seriously—"that doesn't apply to me." Well over fifty percent of everyone that I spoke with had or had had either injury, blisters or both including my own bout of hip issues. Almost all of them could have been prevented.

Some examples that I observed and from conversation with those suffering: sprains, tendonitis, plantar fasciitis and torn cartilage were usually a result of hiking too far, too quickly with disregard for terrain. Contributing factors included overweight backpack, previous injuries, ill-fitted shoes and miss-use of trekking poles. It became a mantra to hear, "I hiked at home and didn't have this problem." Of course not, none of us had hiked every day—walking six hundred miles across constantly changing terrain is a different experience altogether. Another reprise was, "That old football injury hasn't flared up in years. I thought I was over it."

Many injuries were suffered by people who appeared athletic, healthy and falsely encouraged with memories of high school and college sport achievements. They started out walking at least twenty-five miles per day. Many bragged and competed with friends for thirty and even forty mile days. Body parts soon began to fail—sprains, knees, tendons, backs and feet were in full protest. I know that I am climbing in the pulpit here—so forgive me—if you plan to hike or go on an extended walking pilgrimage—listen up.

Start slowly with maybe eight to ten miles each day; gradually increase by two miles daily until you reach your goal. Listen to your body, take off shoes and socks during coffee breaks—let your feet know that you appreciate the hard work that they are doing. Be mindful to the path and it will become your best teacher. Take the time to stop at streams and waterfalls—dangle your feet in the water. Stop and watch farmers care for their crops. Breathe in the air of any moment. Does it say, "I am wheat" or, "I am the sweet mustiness of grapes ready for harvest?" On the camino, villages are so frequent that almost any schedule can be accommodated with the sanctuary of clean albergues and hot food. Pilgrimage is not a marathon.

Backpacks should weigh no more than ten percent of body weight or less. Excess weight of any amount puts serious stress on the knees. The force exerted on the knees is three to six times the added weight. A twenty pound backpack is adding sixty to one hundred twenty pounds per step on the knees depending on whether you are on flat or downhill grade. Injury can come quickly to the knees if the walker locks them going downhill. Walk downhill with the knees flexed using a zigzag or S pattern. On narrow paths it helps if I walk sideways. One day on a very steep and narrow hillside a young man passed me with such speed that I thought he was a large chimpanzee. He had lowered his body and used a "monkey-walk" style to get down the mountain. His legs remained bowed and flared out to the sides as he scrambled out of sight.

Another large help to the knees is to use trekking poles—not one, but two. Many hikers, especially on the camino, aspire to appear as pilgrims in medieval times—with a staff, cane or pole in one hand. In fact there are roadside stands where villagers sell handmade staffs along the entire journey. One staff creates a lopsided, unbalanced posture which can result in sore shoulders, spine displacements and other discomfort. Worse still one knee is always being neglected even if the staff is switched back and forth between hands. Learn to use two poles and it will relieve the knees—twenty pounds for each and every step.

Almost everyone that I spoke with had or had had blisters. One young college girl from Boston sat crying on the roadside. She cradled a blood red foot with large patches of skin missing. A quick glance at her shoes and socks told why. The shoes were low topped reinforced canvas/leather with thin soles and no arch support. She brought the shoes because they were loose and comfortable. She had not considered that her feet would slide and rub as she walked over hills and rocks. The pretty socks she wore were what she always used at home—thin cotton.

First and foremost for long walks, treks or hikes, experts agree, start with the socks. Hiking socks should be heavy, fit well, not bunch up and preferably, wool. It is even better if you use a thin liner which should fit well with no bunching and made of wool or a synthetic material such as polypropylene. Feet sweat—a lot. The liner wicks the perspiration away from the foot into the wool sock. Cotton socks hold moisture, bunch up, and slowly steam the foot in its own sweat. The bunching creates ridges which rub the hot skin into blisters.

I offered companionship and assistance until the next village where my suffering friend could receive emergency care. She accepted my arm, wiped away the tears and said, "I was just trying to keep up with my friends. I didn't want to fall behind and be by myself." At what price, I thought.

Hiking boots whether high or low top should be tried on with the hiking socks you plan to use. If you decide to use a well-worn pair of boots that are old friends, they should fit comfortably tight over the socks. Lose shoes will cause blisters faster than anything else. The constant rhythm of feet sliding inside a hot sweaty shoe is a recipe for disaster. If you purchase new hiking boots, they must pass the sock criteria and be broken in while wearing the correct socks. Look for sturdy construction in a supple material that conforms to the natural shape of the foot. Thick soles that are cushioned to absorb impact will make for happier legs and spine. I walked with a young man who was wearing hiking shoes that had been loaned to him by a friend. He was not walking. He was limping. "They looked nice and I thought the loose fit would be good," he said. He had to spend three day in Burgos recuperating with medical care.

Even under the best of conditions with the correct shoes and socks, hot spots can and do occur. At the very first sign of discomfort, stop, take off your shoes and socks, dry your feet and let them cool down. Then use mole skin or a water resistant Band-Aid to cover the irritated area.

A popular product sold in the UK and all along the camino is called Compede. It is an excellent heavy, padded bandage which will last for a few days, even in the shower. I do not advise using it over blisters. I saw many young hikers remove their Compede bandages with skin attached—not a pretty sight. Compede works great when applied over hot spots to prevent blistering. The most effective treatment when blisters had already formed was to drain the water by using a needle and covering it with a nonstick Band-Aid. Additional surgical tape could then be used to secure the Band-Aid so it would not bunch or slip off while walking.

Hiking any lengthy trail across woodlands, mountains and lush valleys can become a life changing event that will release stress and many fears. At times it can even take us to the summit of spiritual awakening. It is complete folly to pack the old demons of hurry and the confidence of imagined physical abilities. You may want to walk twenty miles but if your body is uncomfortable at ten miles, stop. You may not have reached the destination but you will have learned the teaching of the way.

Personally, I was not walking the Camino de Santiago to prove that I could do it or to arrive at my destination in so many days or weeks. I was walking the path to learn to submit, to accept the teaching of each moment and to listen to my body. Listening to my body was something I obviously had to learn. The lesson of my aching hip should have and could have been addressed much earlier than it was. Somehow, I knew that I was still a cocoon—perhaps walking the Camino would teach me to emerge and become the butterfly. Pilgrimage is about surrender, not conquest.

"It's not the road that wears you out—it's the grain of sand in your shoe." ~Arabian proverb

6

TALKING WITH CATS

*Your purpose in life is to find your purpose and
give your whole heart and soul to it.*
~Buddha

World travelers agree that some cities start telling their stories the moment they arrive. The personality is open; it welcomes us and magically invites us to its inner soul. "Walk my streets, smell the aromas—sit, eat and drink deeply—explore my history and know my people. Once upon a time you were one of them," it whispers.

And so it was with Belorado. Like so many on the camino, this town has been occupied since early Roman times and has been a prosperous Christian community since the tenth century. Ruins of a castle crowned the hill as I entered the town on the east side. Sitting on a cobblestone street under the cascading ruins was the Church of Santa Maria, at one time a chapel of the castle. The original parish hostel that adjoins the church still welcomes pilgrims into its extended family. The old buildings well weathered timbers and creaky narrow stairwell had the charm of a grandmother's attic.

A red cabaret table with a few chairs sat on the apron in front of the hostel and to the left of the old church a vertical limestone cliff rose to support the castle ruins. Cave dwellings that once housed numerous hermits lined the cliffs as silent reminders of a Christian tradition, common from the third century through medieval times. Saint Paul of Thebes, who lived a monastic life as a hermit in the desert is generally considered the first Christian to do so. Belorado historians claim that at least two hermits who lived in these caves were martyred there.

I crossed over the bridge on the Rio Tiron into the town proper where a spacious plaza mayor was lined with restaurants, bars and merchants selling local cheeses, sausages and the wares to supply almost any requirement. A handsome thick stone medieval arcade framed the weathered cobblestone people's square with an inviting charm.

Sitting at one of the café tables was Sarah, a pilgrim from Holland. We had visited in albergues and on the camino previously but her long days and fast stride excluded me as a walking partner. It soon became apparent why I was able to catch up. Her legs were swollen and so painful her face contorted in a grimace every time she moved them. She had stopped to rest and find medical help. I marveled at Sarah's spirit, sense of humor and determination to get well. "I am going to meet my husband in Santiago de Compostela where we will celebrate our wedding anniversary," she said, with laughter and conviction. "I may have to take a bus part way until these legs heal but I will get there."

Down a short side street from the plaza sat a second albergue, different from my choice this night. It was private, modern and popular with the young, fast crowd. An orderly queue had formed much earlier—they were quick to inform newcomers that the hostel only had sixty bunks and there were sixty pilgrims in line. The group took turns leaving for coffee and pastries while a backpack remained to hold their position in line.

I soon learned to avoid the "fast crowd" and where they stayed. On the way into towns they would speed walk past the slower walkers such as me in order to secure a more favorable position in line. They wanted to be among the first in order to get a bottom bunk, first in the shower (hot water), and first on the computers for web access. Another perk of early arrival was an electrical outlet for charging ubiquitous iPhones.

Many of the girls carried hair dryers in their backpacks that were already too heavy. In order to maintain a fashion statement on the camino, they also vied to be first at the laundry facilities. For some, clothes and hair still mattered.

The fast crowd was fast. They were out of bed and on the road at five a.m. rather than comply with the posted request to remain in bed and quiet until six. Conversations were peppered with discussions on how far they would walk the next day and previous records set. They walked in groups of two or more and talked incessantly to each other. I was such a slow old turtle that the crackle of human voice would have the doppler affect as they came from behind and passed in a blur. I was saddened to see the power of peer pressure as many were limping in pain to keep up. Later on, the injured fell out for medical care and recuperation or, as often was the case, they took a bus or train to an airport for evacuation home. Their journey ended in disappointment—not, as hoped, a pilgrimage across a land of myth, mystery, history and self-discovery.

Fortunately the camino is six hundred miles long and that's a lot of space to be alone in. There were days where I saw no one for several hours at a time. Most of the early groups would be dispersed well ahead leaving stragglers and fast trekkers from town's further back to catch up. Sometimes they would slow down to chat and share stories before resuming a pace that was going somewhere far beyond my humble goal.

Once a tall, handsome Korean man came abreast and we nodded to each other as he slowed down to my pace.

We continued in silence for a few steps when he turned to me and said "Sir, may I ask you a question?"

"Yes, of course," I answered.

"How old are you?" he inquired.

It was two months until my next birthday so I lied to him wanting to sound as old and wise as possible. "Seventy-two," I answered.

Silence followed as he stroked a bearded, bronze chin. "Ah . . . in my country you would be much older," he said.

My new friend had in the naiveté's English just handed me the finest put-down ever. My laughter alerted him that maybe he had said something incorrect.

"Is that a bad thing, sir?"

"No, I am unable to guess the ages of Asian friends, because to us, you all look much younger than you are."

"How old do you think I am?" he asked.

"Maybe twenty-five or twenty-eight at the most," I said.

His big smile opened into a chuckle as he lowered his head in a blush, "Really . . . no sir, I am thirty-five already."

As I returned to the albergue from the plaza I stopped on the bridge to admire the tableau of Santa Maria, the hermit caves and castle that lay before me. There in the golden light of the setting sun was a pair of storks. They were perched on a nest that was over eight feet across and equally deep. Its twig construction folded around the top of the old bell tower as though a master architect had designed it.

The weather changed dramatically overnight. High winds, temperature in the low sixties and light rain escorted me out of Belorado as my path began a steady climb towards VillaFranca Montes De Oca. I explored three small villages along the way, visiting their churches and admiring the ruins, imagining the stories they could tell. In Villambistia I meditated in the old church of San Roque which had a lovely sixteenth century retablo. On the way out of the village an inviting rest stop appeared as just the perfect place to let my feet breathe some clean country air. A handsome short-haired tabby came over and sat down near my feet. "Good morning pilgrim," he said.

An imagination is an excellent gift to have but it can become quite scary when unchecked. Perhaps other pilgrims started speaking with animals after long periods alone on the camino—something I needed to inquire into. My new friend angled his head to better gaze directly at me as though he was waiting for a reply.

"Hello, what's your name?" I said out loud.

"Carlos," he continued, "Thank you for speaking with me. Most pilgrims do not trust their gift to hear my thoughts as you do."

"I am excited to meet you, Carlos. In fact I live with a tabby Manx, named Max, in the United States. He looks very much like you but he has no tail."

"What happened to his tail?" Carlos inquired with wide-eyed alarm.

"Manx cats come from the British Isle of Man and are born with no tail. It has always been that way since they were discovered several hundred years ago," I told him.

Carlos shifted his feet a wee bit and seemed amused that my thoughts were trying hard to convince me that I was making up our conversation. People don't talk to cats—It is just my imagination, the little voice inside my head pleaded.

"Don't you talk with Max," he asked.

"Yes, all the time but somehow that seems different. I supply the words and imagine what his reply may be. I actually hear you in my head, not in my ears," I told him.

"Max is speaking with you also but you do not trust your gift and blame your imagination. Here on the Camino you are in a different level of receptivity and you are more open to 'hearing' the thoughts and vibrations of other living creatures," Carlos replied with all the wisdom of a feline Yoda.

I relaxed into the old wooden bench and waited—I was hungry to hear more. Carlos stroked long white whiskers with one paw and continued, "No one in the village speaks with me. Even the other cats do not speak as you and I do. We follow our basic needs of hunger, shelter and sex but we do not speak of it. That is why I come to this bench in search of a human who can trust the voice and ear within.

"When I was a kitten I ran away from my mother to come to this place. No reason, I was just curious. An old man came and sat just where you are sitting on that very bench. He shared the gift with me—we had no problem 'hearing' each other. He said that all creatures are one in their source of energy and that it was perfectly natural to communicate with each other. I was so happy that I wanted to leave with him. He picked me up, hugged me close to a big thumping chest and said that I must remain here. I should wait and help others find their gift. It has been a very long time that I have waited. Many pilgrims come to this bench; very few know the language of all beings. Thank you. It takes wisdom to trust and accept a gift."

Carlos turned and walked away, head held high, eyes darting with a little twitch in the last four inches of his tail. "Hey, come back let's talk some more," I called.

"There will be others," was the last I heard as he disappeared into the nearby shrubbery. For some reason I felt tears on my cheeks. Perhaps, it was the longing for Max and the future conversations we would have. Carlos had awakened the gift of my childhood.

I grew up on a big farm in the rolling hills of West Virginia. As a ward of elderly grandparents, life was severe with hard work and lots of discipline to replace love. I did find love, compassion and understanding but it was from the animals and they became my real family. After my grandparents died, I ran. I ran to other states, other countries and into the arms of the modern world that said, "You can't talk to animals," and I believed them—until today. Chief Dan George said, "If you talk with the animals they will talk with you and you will know each other. If you do not talk with them you will not know them and what you do not know you will fear. What man fears, man destroys."

The earthen path continued through woodlands of pine and oak for another three miles before crossing the Rio Oca and turning into the first of several French settled villages along the camino. VillaFranca Montes De Oca (the French village at Goose Mountains) sits along the Oca River where a pre-Roman Iron Age settlement began as early as seven hundred B.C.E. The city was destroyed in the eighth century by the Moors and didn't recover until the eleventh century. On this night I was quartered in the lovely modern Albergue San Anton. The next day I faced the wall of mountains hovering over the western side of the village. I would have to pass over three mountains topping out at 3773 feet before coming down to St. Juan de Ortega.

"Some people talk to animals. Not many listen though. That's the problem." ~A.A. Milne, *Winnie-the-Pooh*

7

PIT OF BONES

*As a single footstep will not make a path on the earth,
So a single thought will not make a pathway in the mind.
To make a deep physical path, we walk again and again.
To make a deep mental path,
We must think over and over the kind of thought,
We wish to dominate our lives.*
~Henry David Thoreau, *Walden*

The first hour of climbing the Montes De Oca was steep through a forest of oak trees. The lush dark green foliage formed a canopy over large ferns that were waist high. The misty path was eerily silent as oak gave way to stately pine and the dense undergrowth of dew laden ferns grew taller still. Near the summit the pines thinned out into frequent meadows. The air was fragrant with heather, broom, wildflower and large bushes covered with small yellow flowers similar to forsythia.

I had not planned for the weather—after all this was June. What I did have was on my body, including a long sleeve synthetic pullover, a sweater and a nylon windbreaker. Three layers of clothing, thin driving gloves and a cotton hat were no defense to the forty degree weather and strong gusts of wind. Norwegians like to say that "there is no bad weather—only bad clothing." I got the message. The wind chill must have been close to freezing as I struggled to not tumble down the hillside. Three peaks and two valleys later I began the steep, narrow descent into San Juan de Ortega.

San Juan was not to be my overnight sanctuary but it was a welcome rest after the chilling seven mile slog across the mountains. San Juan (1080), a disciple of Santo Domingo, also became known for service to the pilgrims of Santiago. When his mentor died, Juan went on pilgrimage to the Holy Land and on the return he was shipwrecked. He prayed to a relic promising to dedicate his life to the service of pilgrims if he were to be saved. Like Santo Domingo, the myths and miracles attributed to San Juan are the stuff of a good read. He took the name Ortega which is Spanish for thistle or nettle. The village grew around the church of his namesake where he was buried in 1163.

Agés is a small village of less than two hundred people just two miles west of San Juan. There I rested for the night with plans to arrive in Atapuerca early the next morning. I suppose that one thousand years should give any village an opportunity to have its fourteen minutes of fame or infamy. In 1054 at the battle of Atapuerca, King Fernando I of Castile killed his brother King Don Garcia of Navarra. Don Garcia's remains were interred at the local Agés church of Santa Eulalie. The royal body gave prestige to the church and town until the corpse was removed to the Royal Pantheon in Najera. They did manage to retain the king's entrails which remain—in a reliquary at the church.

Agés may be a small town but it has three welcoming hostels and restaurants to pamper pilgrims. I rushed through a shower at the clean well-managed Municipal Albergue to make the afternoon meal at La Taberna Bar and Restaurant. It is amazing how a stew of lentils, followed with OssoBuco, local wine and a warm apple tart can restore a tired pilgrim.

Atapuerca is where many of our European ancestors came from. For millennia this historic valley pass has connected the Iberian Peninsula to France, to the Mediterranean Sea, and via the Duero Valley, to the Atlantic Ocean. The same passageway was followed by the Roman

Roads and later the pilgrimage route to Santiago de Compostela. The Archeological Site of Atapuerca has been designated a UNESCO World Heritage Site.

Discoveries in this ancient cave system have pushed back the arrival of humans in Europe to 1.2 million years ago. Fragments of jawbone and teeth that belonged to Homo erectus were found in the "Pit of the Elephant" and confirm the estimate with a minimum of 1.1 million years. That is 500,000 years earlier than estimates from sites elsewhere in Europe. One of several amazing discoveries at Atapuerca was in the cave known as the "Pit of Bones." More than sixteen hundred human fossils, including nearly complete skulls are estimated to be at least 300,000 years old and some are believed to be double that. The skulls brain capacities suggest several traits within the range of both Neanderthals and modern humans.

I arrived on the plains of Atapuerca in the mists and dew of early morning, well before the official reception area would start receiving the herds of tourists and buses from nearby Burgos. I was content to stand on the pilgrim's path, gaze over the fields and faraway mountains and know that I was walking in the footsteps of my ancestors. The success of their journey was confirmed by my presence—retracing, remembering. I drank deeply of the brisk morning air. My senses were alive as never before. Some primal gene awoke, smelled the campfire and joined the hunt.

The camino has been pushed to the most difficult and extreme limits of acceptability when entering the sprawling city of Burgos. To arrive in the historic city center where pilgrims can sleep in monuments of respectability, they must first navigate a minefield of industrial blight. "Modern Progress" has rerouted the Camino around the huge industrial airport complex forcing walkers to follow the high wire-fenced compound on both the east and south side. There is a relentless (and successful, I might add) attempt to hide the camino in trash filled alleys and industrial backyards. I walked through five miles of this to arrive at the city center.

My body was angry, exhausted and racked with pain. The backpack dug into sweat drenched shoulders, the right hip was failing, both knees hurt and my left foot had developed plantar fasciitis. I was walking like a robot on an expired battery when I dragged up to the reception of La Casa del Cubo, a haven of hospitality and sanctuary. I had just walked fourteen miles in eight and a half hours through the worst of conditions.

La Casa Del Cubo is an architectural masterpiece of six modern floors embraced with a sixteenth century façade. If pilgrim refuges on the camino were to be given stars, this one would get five. Funded and operated by The Friends of The Camino de Santiago, this location has all services. The bunks are arranged in rooms of four with lockers, reading lights and outlets at each location. Lounges, vending machines, laundry facilities, internet and efficient elevators help weary bodies like mine to relax and recuperate from the punishing entry into the city. Perhaps, this was what early medieval pilgrims felt like when they endured similar hardships and found sanctuary. "Let go and accept things as they are," I thought.

Accept and let go. That thought started a chain reaction in examining possibilities available. My body had been pushed to the max and needed time to rest and recuperate. What better place than Burgos—the city of El Cid and the second largest cathedral in all of Spain. My imagination started to plan an exploration of the town: the promenade along the river, Santa Maria square and hot chocolate with churros. Yes, I would take two more days to become friends with Burgos, my new home to explore.

My friend from the Netherlands was sitting at a sidewalk bar as I walked through the Plaza Mayor. She had taken a bus from Belorado to recover here where better medical services were available. "My legs are much better and I will return to the camino tomorrow morning." There was excitement in her voice as Sarah chatted about her recovery and plans to start walking again. "I was fortunate to have found a pensión near here. It has a balcony and a market on the corner for only twenty Euros a day. It has become like home so much that I hate to leave it," she continued. "Most fortunate for me, it is exactly what I am looking for," I replied. The wisdom to stay had just been confirmed.

The old historic heart of Burgos—now a World Heritage Site, lies on the eastern bank of the Rio Arlanzon. Few cities have the number of monuments, churches, and architectural jewels to explore as historic

Burgos. It is a gracious old queen who charms with wide plazas, gothic arcades, wide park-lined pedestrian promenades, magnificence Gothic city gate and one of the most beautiful cathedrals in all Christendom. Excellent restaurants, cafes and bars spill out onto large cobblestone plazas rimmed with Gothic arcades and arched portals. Small grocers, bakeries and craft shops filled every corner of the twisty cobblestone streets. The eye is constantly delighted and teased with colorful displays of pastries, fresh fruits and vegetables, and charcuterie ceilings hung with Spanish Serrano hams and Morcillo sausages. Merchants proudly displayed their wares in meticulously arranged sidewalk stands—one grocer was vainly trying to corral a basket of restless snails.

I needed two days to just get an overview of historic Burgos. The immense cathedral barely revealed itself during my four hour visit. Few buildings on earth have compressed so much architectural wonder into one site. The fine stone work rises on a forest of majestic columns that flow into leafy filigree surrounds that embrace twenty-one church-sized chapels. Every medieval art style is here but the viewer must focus to appreciate it. When seen as a continuous tableau, one is overwhelmed.

As a whole, the architecture was intended to inspire worshipers with awe and a sense of wonder. God surely was here. With sunlight streaming through walls of jewel-like leaded stained glass and the sound of a thunderous ornate organ—He was manifest. Burgos deserves more time than most pilgrims can give. Fortunately, the camino had become my teacher. "When you're free to flow as water, you're free to communicate naturally—Information is exchanged, and knowledge advances in a way that benefits everyone." ~Wayne W. Dyer

Under the crossing of the transept near the main altar rests the tombs of the Count Rodrigo Diaz de Vivar and his wife Doña Jimena. Most of us know him by his Muslim title of respect, El Cid. To Burgos, the Cid is their legendary son and noble warrior-knight. He deftly survived allegiance to warring brother kings in the eleventh century and achieved glory by recovering Valencia from the Moors. He died there in 1099. His body was returned to Burgos in 1921. A heroic statue of the Cid on horseback greets all who cross the San Pablo Bridge to enter the old city gates.

W. Lee Nichols

While having breakfast on the grand promenade overlooking the fanciful topiary, I purchased a European edition of *Newsweek*. The cover story in very large typeface heralded *"End of the Euro."* As I pondered the impending doom, a gentleman attired in custom tailored suit, crisp shirt, handsome tie and designer shoes sauntered by. He stopped at one of the rose bushes lining the sidewalk, pulled a stem with a specimen bloom to his nose, closed his eyes and for several moments—time stood still, as he breathed deeply of the blooms fragrant essence. Disaster sells in the news but to some there is still love and the aroma of roses.

I began to understand that Burgos was a city that still smelled the roses. People did not rush about in a hurry to confirm their self-assured importance. Even traffic on the commercial side of the river flowed rather than surged. There was no problem or concern for citizens to wade through oncoming vehicles mid-block. Sunlight filtered through the canopy of ancient trees to create shafts of sun and shadow on the wide sidewalk. A stream of old men, nannies with prams, children in crisp school uniforms, and seemingly, the whole community strolled underneath. One lone leaf left home from a great sycamore tree and it too, sailed along just above their heads, an air ship suspended on an enchanted breeze. People were greeting each other with an openness and animation that is rare in our western twenty-first century lifestyle. I awakened to the city's charms, this was real magic.

At no time was this more obvious than that evening when I sat at the premiere chocolatier's café for hot chocolate and churros. Café Ibanez is "the place" to go in Burgos for one of Spain's great delicacies. Here, the chocolate is dark, almost as thick as pudding, incredibly intense without a hint of bitterness, and barely sweet. The churros are long, ridged, finger sized fried pastries that are served hot and sprinkled with sugar. When dunked into the hot creamy chocolate, the churro becomes coated with the glossy mixture and without a drip; it holds form until received by anxious lips. Eyes close, there are no words, and the hushed café enters into a world of ecstasy. Sometimes the slightest of sighs will escape the closed lips of novitiates. Let disaster strike somewhere else.

I celebrated my last day in Burgos with a dinner of the regional specialty, Roast Suckling Pig. It was sublime in sweetness and texture with no appearance of fat. The chef had added some pine boughs to the wood fired oven, imparting a perfume to the meat similar to that of rosemary. Fortunately, my departure from vegetarian to a meat based diet a few months earlier was an inspired decision. Many pilgrims were having difficulty finding adequate nutrition and often found themselves salivating at my table. Spain is famous for meat, potatoes and wine.

For over one thousand years kings, nobles, princes of the church and many common men (some who became saints) have stamped the Camino de Santiago with an indelible seal of hospitality. Every city and village has monuments, churches, monasteries, nunneries, castles, hostels and hospitals that were built to house, and feed, and care for the pilgrims that passed through their gates.

In 1195, King Alfonso VIII founded the Hospitál del Rey (Hospice of the King) in the heart of Burgos. Later, Alfonso X, authored sweeping legislation that would govern the hospice and inspire similar decrees the entire length of the Camino Francés. It decreed that all pilgrims, men and women, were to be given shelter, food and beverage; and they were to be provided good beds, clean linen and care. Sick pilgrims were to be nursed, nourished and given all that they might need in order to recover and resume their pilgrimage.

For most people, especially Americans, it is difficult to understand such hospitality and how it became and remains the signature DNA of the camino. King Alfonso's legislation was not unique. In fact, if anything it is the template for all founding documents of the villages and cities on the French Way. That twelfth century symbol of hospitality, the Burgos Hospitàl del Rey, still stands and is the Faculty of Law.

When we listen, the universe seems to favor those that let go of their control buttons and allow themselves to be in the moment. My journey had acquired a guide—the more I surrendered, the more magical the pilgrimage became. As I passed through the Plaza Major that evening a pharmacy seemed to invite me in. I explained to the pharmacist my hip and rash problems, hoping she could recommend something. I did not know that it was a homeopathic pharmacy until the kind lady brought out herbal creams and explained their traditions and use. I am frequently reminded, "Suffering is optional." I had almost immediate relief—tomorrow the way would be easier.

8

ALIVE & WELL

Enlightenment is a state of being. Like all states of being it is indescribable. It is a common misconception (literally) to mistake the description of a state of being for the state itself.
~Gary Zukav, *the Dancing Wu Li Masters*

Where are the cameras and the director calling "action?" Rabe de las Calzadas must be the model for Spanish medieval movie sets. There are no Coke signs or any modern intrusion into this dreamy little village of some two hundred folks. It sits upon a mesa, overlooking farms of grain and sheep. The village square centers a compound of aged buildings in sun washed monochrome. The thirteenth century Iglesia de Santa Marina, a handsome palace with towers, the albergues and two story homes are all united in sepia toned, aged sandstone and brick. Red tile roofs add the only color.

There are two quaint albergues so I chose the smaller which had only eight beds. The Albergue Hospital de Peregrinos Santa Marina y Santiago is owned and run by a couple from northern Europe. The madame turned out to be the most eccentric and odd individual that

I encountered on the entire pilgrimage. Eight of us had gathered on the porch to wait the appointed hour she would open. Upon opening the door, madame became the grand inquisitor and lecturer on camino protocol. In her eyes we all needed discipline, nurturing and proper tuck-ins at bed time. Every night she could turn a house full of pilgrims into "her little family."

She asked that we come inside and register, one at a time. I had waited the longest and as such was elected to stick my head in the oven first.

"Your passport is bogus, it is not filled out properly, are you a tourist trying to pass as a pilgrim?" she scolded. There was no time allowed for answers. "You will take dinner . . . it is extra" she continued.

I jumped in, "I do not eat dinner—I only take two meals each day," and quickly added, "I sometimes get acid reflux if I eat late so I only take fruit and tea after five p.m."

She countered, "If you don't take dinner, you will not be able to walk the camino. There . . . now that is proof that you are a tourist. You could not have walked here as a pilgrim with no dinner last night."

Somehow, I had been caught in a Stephen King novel and felt a desperate urge to leave before my ankles were broken.

In a total about face, she stood up, pointed an accusing finger and demanded, "You go upstairs, take a shower and come down so I can inspect your feet. Tonight I will make you a dinner that will not cause the acid reflux."

My friends waiting on the porch told me later that I ran out the door, backpack and hat in hand as though I had seen a ghost. "Worse than that, much worse," I replied.

Across the plaza stood the larger hostel with twenty-four beds, the Albergue Liberanos Domine. The charming young owners created a fine welcome as I was shown to a sweet smelling room with a screen on the open window. A cool breeze floated in from the wheat fields on the mesa. My thoughts drifted to what today's lesson might have been. "Why didn't I come here first? Is one place teaching me to recognize resistance and the other flow?"

Soon I was doing laundry. "Let me finish your laundry—I will hang it out in the sunshine while you enjoy lunch at the bar down the hill," said the gentlest of voices. My hostess who had been watching the progress of my domestic efforts took over loading the machine. Wow, flow sure takes some quick turns, I thought. I could have been standing at attention, having my feet inspected.

"By watching the mechanics of the mind, you step out of its resistance patterns, and you can then allow the present moment to be." ~Eckhart Tolle, *the Power of Now*. I stepped outside the albergue during first light of morning. That day was like no other. To first appearance it was just a tranquil village scene on the camino. I breathed deeply, searching the air-born molecules for a clue. The difference was inside me, I was no longer a separate entity observing. I felt transparent and totally part of this village, the countryside and beyond—forever. I was aware, awake and in that moment everything was one. A shepherd was herding his sheep across the misty valley; close by a barn door opened. A farmer drove his tractor out onto the cobblestone street and down the hill, his large German shepherd following—sniffing road side weeds as he trotted along. "So this is what it's like to be alive."

I had known moments like this as a child but only in the fields, meadows and mountains when I was alone. During those days, the animals would come to me with total acceptance and offer their friendship. They would quickly shy away when my grandfather or one of the farm hands was around. It was as if we didn't want to get caught talking to each other. They had very good reasons to fear and I shared that fear. The lives of our horses, cattle, sheep and poultry were expendable and in a boys mind; there go I. Animals were a mere commodity, openly traded and consumed. It was painful to be their friend and unable to defend their right to happiness and life. "It is just the way things are—you're too sensitive," my grandmother would say. "He's a worthless sissy," chimed in my grandfather.

Pain can last a lifetime but it also can be released in a moment's flash of awareness. When I accepted the happiness and joy of oneness with the moment—I also accepted myself. I accepted my right to be happy—I was worthy of the wisdom that dwelled within. Actually, I was humbled by my new awareness. I no longer had to defend the man behind the mask.

The five mile hike to Hornillos Del Camino led across what many call "Spain's great cereal bowl." Before me laid a giant quilt of green and tan fields planted in oats, barley and wheat. Directly in my path was the first large meseta. In the plains of western United States similar flat topped hills are called mesas. Spain's northwest plains have many of these giants that are farmed on the slopes and tops. It would take my entire morning walk just to cross one 3117 foot tall meseta. On the other side lay Hornillos.

Red patio tables and metal folding chairs spilled out across the small plaza and into the main road with no regard for traffic. The consensus was that no one should be going so fast that a chair couldn't be moved. The local dogs felt the same way. I joined a jovial rag-tag group of pilgrims who seemed to have arrived at the same conclusion. There was no reason to hurry; I could go on to the next village or not. I visited with several groups and individuals—the camaraderie was amazing. These were new acquaintances but they were like old friends. Suddenly I understood, "It's me that has changed and opened up. Perhaps these folks have always been who they are."

Mike, a businessman from Manchester had been on the camino for two weeks. He sat with his socks off, enjoying a local brew while massaging his feet. "I don't know how, but I'm supposed to go back next week and I don't want to," he told me. "It's just now that I'm starting to feel the pressure lift—it's time to go back to work. What I really would like to do is fly my teenage daughter over and have her finish the camino with me. She is in college and this may be our last opportunity to have a long father-daughter get-together."

I was moved that Mike was so open with me, sharing his personal thoughts. "Why don't you arrange for more time off and call your daughter. Make the arrangements for her to meet you in Leon. They have a large airport," I encouraged.

"That's why I am sitting here and not walking—lots to mull over," he answered.

"I'm sure that you'll make the correct decision," I told him.

A young couple from Liverpool called me over and asked to see my camino guidebook. They had been hiking without one and were wondering about the mileage to the next few villages. "How far do you want to go?" I inquired. "We don't know," Penny said. "We just walk until we can't go any further and stop. Sometimes we walk until after dark in order to find a village." She laughed with an infectious throaty chuckle that would have made any whisky baritone proud.

Penny ground the half smoked cigarette butt into the cobblestones as though it were a scorpion. She continued while lighting another, "We saw this movie one night. It's called *The Way*. We must have been a little high because the next day we said 'let's do it.' The movie is about this very road, the camino. So here we are." She laughed with large brown eyes that smile so much they have permanent happy crow's feet.

"I've seen it and it's a good movie. I'm glad you were inspired to come," I told her. "My guide book is simply called, *A Pilgrim's Guide to the Camino de Santiago*. It is written by John Brierley and is considered by many, myself included, to be the 'Camino Bible.' You will be able to buy one in Leon at bookstores."

She wrote down the information, gave me a big hug and marched off with her silent companion in tow.

I joined a young man leaning against the Taberna wall, backpack on the street beside him. He seemed to take pleasure in being a people watcher. "Interesting two-some you were talking to," he drawled.

"Yes, they are a little lost but the Camino has a way with folks. They'll be okay; the road will teach them," I told him. Greg was from the USA but had been working in the Arab Emirates for several years.

"I am a pilot and work for a petroleum conglomerate which brings me to the States and Europe on a regular basis," he said.

"I have irregular blocks of time on my own so I am doing the camino in segments. The first time I walked from Paris to Pamplona. This time I hope to get to Leon. Perhaps next year I will be able to go all the way to Santiago."

"Do you think that you might go all the way to the end of the world—Finesterre, on the Atlantic coast?" I asked.

"Oh yes, most definitely but I will probably take the bus from Santiago rather than walk there—how about you?"

"Yes, I am going to the coast and then maybe some more. I don't know where this journey will lead me," I told him.

Hornillos is no newcomer to the camino. It is just a village of fewer than a hundred inhabitants that goes back to pre-Roman times. The name implies that it may have had a smelting furnace or brick kiln in its early history. The pleasant Albergue Hornillos Del Camino has thirty-two beds with laundry, internet, and kitchen. I was happy to make this my home and become a resident, at least for a day.

After a late afternoon meal at Casa Manolo, I walked around the village and talked with some of the farmers returning from their fields and herds. They were curious where I came from, what life was like in America and how old I was. The elderly are not uncommon on the camino but perhaps curious, nosey ones like me provide an easier opportunity for an exchange. Some of the mud-brick buildings were only fronts on the street. The rear walls had long returned to the earth and the roof tiles recycled. One held tomato plants in bloom and another contained old ceiling beams and weeds.

Returning into town I heard repeated blasts on a car horn. I soon discovered that the disturbance came from a small refrigerated truck. It had parked in the middle of the plaza—on the side painted in bright red script was 'Carnicera' (meat market). Housewives, still in aprons, were rushing out of their homes to buy dinner.

Gloria joined me on the patio for tea and apples that evening. She was a small woman in her late sixties with a tangle of short grey hair. She had retired on May second, sold her car, rented her house in California and arrived on the camino on May twenty-second.

"After the camino I don't know where I'll go next but my plans are to take a few years to go around the world," she calmly declared. "I have no plans to return. To where? The road is my home; the people I meet are my family." I was very happy to meet her and told her how much I admired such a brave journey.

Mike joined me soon after Gloria's visit with a big smile and hearty greeting. "What are you doing here—I thought you were on the road to the next village?" I said.

"I've been on the phone and internet all afternoon." He was bubbling with enthusiasm. "I bit the bullet and called my company; they agreed to give me two more weeks. So, my daughter will join me in Leon. We are going to have so much fun together."

Talking With Cats

"What a happy story Mike, thanks for sharing it." I told him.

"Well, my wife says she will miss me and we have never been separated this long. It's going to be hard on the bank account—but it's only money" He slapped me on the shoulder and headed off to the shower, singing some ditzy tune.

I went to bed thinking about my own family and how much it would mean to have one of them with me. Of course, there would be concessions to be made. We would explore, talk and share but the dynamics would change. It would not be my pilgrimage any longer—it would be ours. Perhaps it is the longing to share that draws each of us deeper to explore the bonds of blood and the depth of our love. My heart is light, feeling secure with the knowledge of those who hold a light on my path.

The next day I headed out to walk six and a half miles across two large mesetas and to enjoy the afternoon and night in Hontanas. After more than three hours on the camino there was no village in sight. I had just crossed the larger 3200 foot meseta which had a good sight line across the plains. Not a building could be seen anywhere. The village showed clearly on my map and guidebook. Could I have taken the wrong road from Hornillos?

As I started down the meseta, a hundred yards ahead sat Hontanas, tucked within a fold so well hidden that one has to be upon it to see it. What a clever protection for a medieval village—let the landscape make it disappear. What my eye did see was another page from history—myth fused with reality—clinging to the weathered meseta's cliff. On the way into the village a stone drinking fountain splashed into its basin where song-birds and doves drank. The town was festive with activity. A poster announced an art show for that very day. Sidewalks were being scrubbed; chefs were cooking just beyond open windows; flower boxes and vines were in full bloom. Every view down side streets, into courtyards and beyond was like a medieval Shangri-La come to life.

I stayed in the converted medieval pilgrim's hospice Albergue Santa Brigida. It has been lovingly transformed into a modern well-appointed hostel without losing a stone of charm or intrigue. The fresh smell of pine ceilings permeated the rooms and modern baths. A fine restaurant with an excellent chef was housed in the front and a large enclosed courtyard with arbor provided refuge for reading and social time. A real advantage to Hontanas is that pilgrims do have choices here and the competition stimulates better places to stay and eat.

How does one describe happiness? Was it the view across the mesetas or perhaps the gentle breeze that entered the room from one window and flowed out the other? Maybe it was the slow cooked pot roast with potatoes roasted in a bed of rosemary—not to mention a velvety flan bathed in its own caramel. For sure the Sangre de Torro red wine contributed to my happiness. The effervescent energy of five fellow peregrinos (pilgrims) as roommates created a lot of spontaneous happiness, laughter, and conversation. None of us had ever met before but that day and evening we were the best of family. Maybe happiness is just the power of being, of accepting and surrendering to the flow of life. Like the breeze—in one window and out the next.

The art show was scheduled for that evening at the parish Church of the Conception. We did not know what to expect but it was a local cultural diversion that we welcomed. We climbed a flight of stairs on the side of the fourteenth century building and stepped into what might have been a cleric's quarters. To me, it looked more like the artist's garret in the opera La Boheme. New age music set the stage as a radiant young woman introduced herself, "I am Nia Peiro, welcome."

The show was to introduce the poetry, craft and soul of an amazing man. Mau Mariani left his native Italy twenty-five years ago to travel the world. He came to the Camino de Santiago and has spent the past twenty years walking and giving his service to the pilgrims on its path. Nia Peiro, also from Italy, who has degrees in the arts, has joined Mau's pilgrimage. Together they travel the Way of Saint James where they serve their fellow pilgrims in the convents, monasteries and albergues. The exhibition highlight was Nia's photography. The haunting and inspirational imagery was of nature, Mau and other pilgrims in unique locations as they walk the camino. She has continued scheduling these joint exhibitions as an offering to fellow pilgrims—to give a new window of seeing and participating in a selfless pilgrimage. The small offerings that they accept for the photos and artifacts assist in continuing their journey.

Their show of photographs "The Camino de Santiago—The Road behind the Shadows" was available for sale in various sizes including greeting cards. Mau had written poetry appropriate to each picture.

The photos were spectacular, sacred in nature and as Mau said, "We hope that they give our fellow pilgrims another set of eyes to see our beloved Way of Saint James." Mau and Nia collect unusual stones, seed pods, and other artifacts of nature as they walk the camino. Those items had been transformed into amulets, talisman and 'sacred' relics also for sale at their shows.

Later our paths crossed a few times. I too witnessed Mau's selfless giving. One time a homeless man from Africa was traveling the camino with his dog. He walked the way as a true medieval pilgrim might—at the mercy of others. In one village as I gave him my spare change he told me that his backpack had torn beyond repair and he was using an old sheet. Later that day I saw Mau buy him a strong new pack. At one of the albergues, Mau was sweeping floors and changing the linen and yet another time he was dressing the blisters on someone's feet. Modern saints abound, we just have to see them (and be them).

9

SUFFERING IS OPTIONAL

*How long the road is. But, for all the time
The journey has already taken, how you have needed
every second of it in order to learn what the road passes by.*
~Dag Hammarskjold, Markings

I descended from the meseta that Hontanas clung to and headed west on a path surrounded with a gentle undulating landscape of grain fields. On the north side of the road, ruins of a twelfth century village lay in silent crumble. The only sizeable remains were those of a church whose stone and brick gave testament to the fragility and temporal existence of all things. I mused on the rigid linear time lines that modern western civilization imposes on daily life. Here on the camino many pilgrims had brought that same framework of clock-time to measure their daily progress.

For most people, our human existence is literally compressed in boxes—measured in time: childhood, education, relationships, success, retirement and dying; all in a straight line—birth to death. How different it must have been for early settlers on this ancient well-trodden path;

they had sundials to measure the day; the moon ruled their months; solstices, equinoxes and the stars divided and determined their years.

Many early tribal cultures such as some Native Americans conceived of time as circular. Their lives entered a spiral of time that taught a connectedness to all things. The circular thinkers were not only of the planet, but of the stars, the cosmos and beyond. Their non-linear universe established a reverence for what they did not know. Within the spiral, all knowledge and wisdom was knowable—it only had to be awakened.

Walking slowly, allowing my body, the weather and villages to determine each day's destination enhanced my awareness of the time continuum. That awareness freed me to experience all past, present and future events in a more objective relativity. Outside of conventional linear time I was free—I no longer "had" to meet any expectations. Living in the "now" allowed each location, bird, flower and sunset to be a revelation of wonder. Philo of Alexandria (20 BCE-50 CE) said, "Today means boundless and inexhaustible eternity. Periods of months and years and of time in general are ideas of men, who calculate by number; but the true name of eternity is today."

Directly ahead lay the ruins of another village that once had been a thriving pilgrim's stop. The camino path passed through the church's center—under the roofless arches of the fourteenth century Convent of San Anton. The complex in the twelfth century included a church, hospice, convent, mill and orchard. The ruins were like an old etching found in a Paris bookshop; beautiful, almost romantic as the grand ribs, towers, and filigreed stonework that once held a magnificent stained glass window embraced my passage. I sat down amidst the great stone bones—still splendid in their decay. I wanted to be quiet and listen to the many stories they might have to tell.

The order, created in France during the eleventh century, was connected to the Egyptian hermit, Saint Anthony or San Anton Abad. He was known as the patron saint of animals—and is often pictured with a pig at his feet. The Anton order was known for their ability to cure a medieval skin disease known as St. Anthony's fire and also leprosy. At its height they administered over 350 hospitals in Europe. A special cross, the Greek letter Tau, was the instrument used in their healing and worship. Here at the ruins and in neighboring villages the large stone Taus stand sentry today, an instrument of faith in God's healing power through love. The order was disbanded in 1787.

One demon continued to plague and annoy an otherwise magical walk through time that day. It was called 'the hip.' The pain caused a bad limp that invited fellow pilgrims to stop and offer assistance—"Are you all right? Can I carry your backpack?" That was not the image that I had of neither myself nor the one I wanted to project. How was I going to become the poster boy for senior citizens? Naturally, I refused help—"this was *my* cross to bear."

I climbed a rise that lead through a small forest where the path was lined with stones. One had been artfully hand lettered in black script. It read "Pain is inevitable. Suffering is optional." For some reason I saw that sign as personal with instructions for me only. I imagined the letters disappearing as I walked away. Maybe new instructions appeared for each pilgrim's malady as they passed by. I was ready to believe in magic stones.

Soon after the sorcerer's stone I hobbled into Castrojeriz, my face tense with pain. The town was terraced on a hillside with steep cobblestone alleys and stairways connecting the various street levels. At the top end of town with a panoramic view of the village and plains below was the Albergue San Esteban. It was located on the top floor above the cultural center directly on the plaza mayor. The hospitalero was standing out front watching my painful arrival. "You, give me your backpack. The doctor's office is across the street—go now," he gently commanded.

I was in the doctor's examining room within fifteen minutes. He was thorough, asking lots of questions while ordering me into various positions—all in Spanish. I had entered the camino without having used Spanish for forty years—I was pleased to pass that day's test. After the exam he asked me to sit at his desk. "You have an inflammation in the hip socket, nothing worse. Take this prescription and in fifteen days try decreasing the dosage until you no longer need to take it." He stood, extending a hand with a sigh, "I would tell you to rest for a few days but I imagine that you will continue on your pilgrimage regardless of what I say—so buen camino."

After a late lunch I returned to the plaza mayor and sat on a bench under the arcade. A sleek black cat strolled over to join me. He sat down near the end of the bench, licked one paw, and stared directly into my face. "How's life?" I opened.

"Lousy, dreary town, rude pilgrims—anything else you want to know?" came his sarcastic reply.

"Excuse me; I thought you might be a smart cat not a smart-ass. How long have you been talking with humans?"

"What's special about that?" Mr. Cat wanted to know. "They're not very intelligent, anyway. You should hear the stupid questions they ask me—the ones that can hear my language, that is. I understand that many species in the universe are intelligent, but most of them are cats.

"Most humans want to know personal details, like how many ladies are in my life, what's sex like for cats, and what do I eat. Mice, I tell them just to watch the disgust on their faces." My new friend continued, "They want to know my name—since we don't use names, I tell them what the shop keepers call me. It's Gatito, Gatita or kitty, kitty, kitty or Vamoose with a swift kick in the ass. Sometimes pilgrims will run off and buy me food at the grocers which is all I wanted anyway. Humans are very easy to train, you know."

"Well, Mr. Cynical Cat—what do you want to talk to humans about?" I asked.

"Quantum Physics," he said and strolled off towards the butcher shop.

10

DEMONS ON THE RIVERBANK

*In the universe,
There are things known,
And things that are unknown,
And in between,
There are doors.*
~William Blake

What a difference a pill makes. With only one day on meds my life was transformed. Soon after leaving Castrojeriz I climbed a steep meseta called Mostelares whose three thousand foot summit became a joy of triumph. Not only was suffering optional, the pain was gone. I discovered walking to be a satisfying art form unto itself—my strides were longer and more confident—I became empowered with the spirit of release. "I had better slow down or be tempted to join the fast crowd," I thought. It was like skiing for the first time.

The departure that morning from Castrojeriz was across marshy flat land surrounding the Odra River. I walked on the old Roman causeway—suspended on long, low stone arches. It led onto a twelfth century stone bridge before heading up the earthen and rock path of the steep Meseta. The Roman solution to the flood cycles of the river was impressive in both construction and esthetic—a lesson worthy of modern urban planners.

Descent from the meseta was on an eighteen percent grade with a view to miles of wheat, barley, and oats—their tall thin stalks chased and herded into great waves by the winds. In the distance lay the village of Itero de la Vega, like an island in a pale green sea. Once again I was walking on the old Roman road where ghosts of its builders cheered me on. In some places the roadbed was eroded with the stones turned at strange angles. I slowed down to imagine the pageant of history that had traveled over those very stones during the past two thousand years. Leagues of legionnaires built it, Roman charioteers inspected it, kings and knights defended it, and a thousand years of pilgrims have streamed over it with blistered feet and a defiant faith. That day, I walked on the same stones.

My companions on portions of today's trek were a mother and daughter from Canada and a young man from Germany. Kirsten, Jackie and Sam had connected earlier and found that their daily goals made for a compatible friendship. They were surprised that I had not teamed up with others and were curious if I were lonely. I was totally surprised at the question as I took being alone to be an advantage and not an emotional hardship. I struggled for words of understanding and diplomacy to avoid offending their sincere charitable offer to "keep me company on this lonely, barren road." When we truly listen to people—we learn that the fears and concerns they project on others are their very own.

I felt challenged to express my personal awareness and joy as a subtle teaching and not a rebuke. I was aware that my three friends were experiencing their own sense of bravery, and though in a different way, they would return home empowered by having taken their own journey. Perhaps an old man along the path would provide a story they could take back—and it would continue to evolve for them. After all,

Talking With Cats

we are but seeds—we never know when someone will take us home and plant us in their garden. When we parted, amid farewell wishes—Kirsten said "You are the luckiest person we have met on the camino. Every night you have a whole new family to share with."

I arrived in Itero de la Vega famished for something familiar—a big plate of comfort food—no three course meal-of-the-day with wine. The private Albergue La Mochila (the backpack) was not ready to receive guests but welcomed me anyway. This tidy well managed hostel on Calle Santa Ana gets my vote for being one of the most hospitable on the Camino. La Mochila is run by two young entrepreneurial women who understand service as a hallmark of success. They flew to the kitchen when I said "hungry" and produced eggs with bacon and potatoes skillet fried in olive oil. A fresh baked baguette and fruit soon had this wolf tamed and happy.

The town of Itero del Castillo sits on the east side of the Rio Pisuerga and Itero de la Vega is on the west side. Villages, estates and churches around the river often start with Itero, a derivation of a medieval term meaning 'fixed stone' or boundary stone, which is what towns along the river, have been for thousands of years. Today the river forms the border between the provinces of Burgos and Palencia—two of the three in the region of Castile and Leon that I will walk through.

Palencia is known as the Tierra de Campos or Land of Fields. It is a vast flat region, fed by rivers and extensive canals that support one of Spain's most fertile agricultural garden belts. Wheat, vegetables and grapes for wine were the dominate crops that lined the camino for many miles and days of walking.

This account is only one old man's personal journal and I make no attempt to turn it into an exhaustive guidebook for the Camino de Santiago. However, I do hope that it speaks directly to pilgrimage and the awakening process of walking. I especially want to reach out to my peers—the 'Baby Boomers.' Many seem to have no plans or dreams about what to do during retirement. As I told my doctors, we must find a way to send a message to our bodies, to our souls and to our families that "It's not over yet." I am sure you've heard the aphorism, "If you can complete your dreams in your lifetime—they're not big enough."

It certainly rings true for me. The alternative is to make busy—tread water—and wait.

It seems like life is always willing to give us another chance when we go in quest of that noble truth 'Who am I.' Once again, at any age, we can become knights in search of the Grail within; we sharpen our senses, live in the moment and summon the courage to do battle with the darkest of foes. And when death comes—and it surely will—we will be released from the dread and fear that shadows those who were life's conscientious objectors or refused the good fight.

Life on earth is a process of metamorphous—we humans do not arrive ready to go. Like the flowers in a beautiful garden, we too start as a seed. Once the transition from seed to plant occurs the promise of its life's purpose appears in the form of a bud—this is but the beginning of what can be. Most of us are exquisite buds in earth's beautiful garden of wonder and magical powers. We are full of dreams, hope and imagination held tightly within. But often we are born and we die as buds—unable to open and become part of the garden's beauty and magic. By awakening to our full potential we fulfill our destiny. We bloom, to become blossoms of hope—empowered with all the wonders of the garden. Greater still, is the legacy of the fertile seeds that will fall to the earth—in the cycle of life blooms a new garden.

Yesterday evening I joined three women on the patio for wine and cheese. Two sisters and their family friend were from Capetown, South Africa. They were happy, well prepared for the camino and joyous about everything. They had come on their pilgrimage to celebrate their father's life—not to mourn him. And celebrate they did.

The next day it was a pleasure to walk with them as the celebration continued with the telling of family events and personal incidents from a bottomless pit of Daddy stories. The laughter was contagious as each story climaxed in squeals of bent-over, leg-slapping humor. The sisters were intent on besting each other as to whose story was the funniest.

"Sorry that I never had a chance to meet Daddy" I said. "I only hope my children have this much fun remembering me. The stories they recall now are about the many times I almost got them killed: There was the attack by bandits in remote Mexico, the climb on dangerous cliffs over shark infested waters in the Virgin Islands, and a few other similar incidents where they have perfect recall. None are funny."

"Tell us some of the things you did to your children and we'll laugh," Virginia encouraged.

The land we walked is the land we were promised: flat, well irrigated farms with tree lined canals for the entire eight and a half miles to Fromista. This was Palencia. The canals were masterpieces of engineering, having been built on raised earthen platforms some forty or fifty feet above the fields. Small trap doors were set at regular intervals into the canal walls. When they were lifted the gravity fed water would rush down concrete sluices into the fields and on into the horizon.

Fromista sits in the center of the richest grain-growing area of all Spain. Caesar came here for the vast wheat fields 2100 years ago, kings and knights shed blood for it throughout medieval history and the land just keeps on giving. The enormous lock on the old Canal de Castilla is awe inspiring and somewhat intimidating since the camino foot traffic must cross it on a small open metal bridge. It was built in the mid-1700s and is a marvel of antiquated cogs, wheels, pulleys and chains that still function to lower and raise the many cascading water levels.

The town of Fromista has become a side show, held hostage by an eleventh century church which attracts hordes of tour buses and school outings. The Iglesia de San Martin is reputed to be the finest example of pure Romanesque architecture in all of the Iberian Peninsula. It was built under the direction of the Navarran King Sancho el Mayor's widow, Doña Mayor. Architects from Jaca were brought in; the large square-cut stones were imported and in 1066 master stone carvers, sculptors, masons and painters set about to create a masterpiece. They did. Even though it has been fully restored and is now a museum, it is splendid.

Many fascinating myths and stories pepper the entire route of the camino and its villages. Most popular among them are the temptations by devils and demons suffered by Saint James and his followers. A sixteenth century retablo at the Iglesia de Santa Maria la Blanca in the village of Villalcazar de Sirga (Village of the Castle of Pilgrimage Way) depicts nine scenes from the life of Santiago. Four of the panels tell of his encounter with the magician Hermogenes and his many demon companions.

The road out of Fromista offered two options. The first and most direct ran parallel to the highway on a new state built earthen track called a *senda*. Seeing no possibility for adventure on what my guidebook said was *soulless and treeless* I choose the longer and more remote tree lined path which followed the Ucieza River. That day I confronted and fought Hermogenes and his demons along the river bank.

The departure for the river trail was at the small village of Poblacion de Campos. Instructions to find the river trail said, "Do not cross the bridge but turn right along road and then turn left along the river." I went a short distance and watched as all the other pilgrims streaming down the camino choose to walk the faster highway route. I thought it odd that no one else had chosen to walk in nature with trees, crystalline murmuring waters and bird-song. Most all guidebooks offer detailed descriptions of alternate routes and certainly my fellow pilgrims knew about the option. The majority proudly carried the same "Camino Bible" as I did.

The riverbank path was hardly worthy of being called a path—more like a narrow service road for the farmers whose crops spread out to the north of the river. Unlike the well-trod camino that I had walked for the past three weeks, this road offered no clue that anyone else had been there for months. The tall grass and weeds were still covered with morning dew and an occasional spider web—nothing had disturbed their tranquility that day—especially a human on foot. I walked back to the side road that led from the bridge and looked for the familiar camino signposts. Perhaps, I had missed the real path, but how? The map clearly showed the route following the river and there was no place for it to be further inland. No signs and no evidence that others had been on the river trail simply meant that they were in a hurry and I was not. I would be the brave one that day and take the path least traveled.

There were lots of trees—at times almost a mini forest so dense that the nearby river would be obscured by the abundant undergrowth. There was also a buffer of trees on the opposite side of the path overlooking the vast acreage of vegetable fields. I was walking down a tunnel, shrouded in a dark stillness. I frequently turned to look over my shoulder—hoping for another pilgrim who could reassure me that they too—had chosen the path of nature. Once, I saw someone, so far back on the trail that they were but a small dark silhouette. I decided to walk slowly in hopes they would catch up.

No one caught up—there was no one behind me—at least no one that I could see. The dark blue-green river became deep and swirling with occasional whirlpools. Often there would be old campsites where I imagined that a fisherman would roast his catch. Suddenly an uncontrollable fear took over my mind. This would be a great place to dispose of a body, it warned.

This was not some small voice whispering caution—it was a thunderous booming voice of doom that screamed of impending disaster. Worse still, it was in control. The more I fought with reason, the stronger the fear became. The voice continued with lurid, graphic details as to how my body would be disposed of and where my gear would be stashed with the killer's ever-growing collection of backpacks. I looked in both directions; maybe I did see someone—someone who was following me behind the tree line. I became desperate and wanted to run.

A small bird about the size of a cardinal sat on a tree nearby. Suddenly she began to sing, the way mother birds sing when she sees a snake. Clearly disturbed, the bird began wildly jumping around on her branch as though she had a warning for someone. I broke free. "Leave me; I will not have demons obstructing my path!" I screamed out loud, startling my little companion to take a hasty flight.

Still shaking from the experience, I started gathering together the reality and facts of my safety and the beauty of my surroundings. I marveled at how doubt about my initial decision had allowed this demon to enter, induce paranoia and take control of my thoughts. For the first time in my life I understood those who cannot escape the dark forces that imprison them in fear. I felt a release of compassion that flowed from me—out across the river, the fields and beyond. I fell to the ground sobbing in joy and humility for the gift that I had just received. Like Santiago, I had passed the test of Hermogenes and his demons.

The struggle on the riverbank became an awakening of all my senses—earth had never been this beautiful. It was as though I had stepped out of a dark stone prison into the garden of paradise. I was filled with the rich, heady aroma of tilled soil—the sweetness of immature wheat bathing in sunlight, the wetness of the river joyfully making its way to the distant sea and the trees and wild flowers—all in saturated color and a master's touch of computer generated imagery. I was part of a multidimensional world, drinking it all in like new wine—and like every day and every moment in mindfulness, for the very first time.

I crossed an ornate wrought iron bridge at Villovieco where the path continued along the other side of the river. I never met another person, pilgrim or otherwise, during the entire six miles. At the Hermitage of Our Lady of the River, the path turned south to rejoin the main Camino de Santiago at Villalcazar. How many others have been led the way of the river trail—and how many have been challenged by fears induced by the legendary magician and his demons?

I arrived in Villalcazar at eleven a.m., yet the village was not ready to receive guests. The two albergues did not open until two p.m.—the bakery said that the bread and rolls would not be out of the oven until later, and a lone tour group dominated the Church of Santa Maria. There was a strange cloud of energy hovering over Villalcazar and I suspected that the wraith of Hermogenes might have returned to continue his teaching of fear. Santiago's life was victorious over this demon—and on this day, I was honored to be sheltered with the lessons of such an exalted teacher. A powerful and wise inner voice told me to continue my pilgrimage—it was just four more miles down the camino to Carrion de Los Condes.

Back on the path to Los Condes, I found an old friend resting against a tree. "Waiting on someone?" I asked. "You," she said as we headed west together. Sharon Rochester, turned seventy that day, and her story of life as a mother, grandmother and pilgrim was heartening in its determination to overcome fears and find her own truth. The path was both timeless and familiar as we entered a city that became one of the highlights of my pilgrimage.

The heart of the village had been taken over with market day. The booths and stalls of ripe red cherries, regional sausages, garden produce and clothing were crammed together on the plaza mayor, down the side streets and sometimes onto the sidewalks. I passed two albergues and hostels but something still led me on. The banners, tents and clothes lines completely hid the signage to the pilgrim facilities but I continued to push my way through. Some voice, some force was directing my feet and legs to keep going. I was being led and knew that I would know it when I saw it.

I did not understand the force that lead me to the great wooden doors of Santa Maria Convent but I felt it when one of the sisters welcomed me with a hug. The twelfth century convent is run today by a small band of Augustine Nuns who have dedicated their lives to serve pilgrims on the camino. As I prepared to leave for lunch, a sister said "Please join us this evening for a little music concert and welcome celebration at 6:30."

Sharon had stopped at the village entrance where she had reservations at the Santa Clara Monastery. I was surprised that we both found the same restaurant for lunch since there were several appealing locations to choose from. She was excited that her private room at the monastery had a large bathtub—a real luxury on the camino. We discussed the extraordinary forces that had led me to take the river trail—not to stay in Villalcazar—and to find the convent. On impulse I said, "Why don't you join me tonight for the music concert at my convent? It will be the perfect occasion to celebrate your birthday."

That evening an audience of pilgrims gathered in the foyer and eventually flowed up the stairs into a standing room only crowd. Five nuns, clad in white habits sat in front of the giant open doors. They each held small instruments of percussion, and some played banjo, guitar and a large ceremonial drum. The setting sun shafted across the plaza, through the open door and across the shoulders of those five glowing angels—as though they might ascend to heaven at any moment.

Music sheets containing the lyrics in four languages were passed around as the nuns led the assembly into a family communion of song and spirit. We were each given time to speak of our personal journey with the nuns translating for the representatives of twenty countries. It was a global family united by powerful personal stories, laughter, music, talent, and the unselfish love of our hosts.

No one was an outsider. There were no prayers, no preaching, no rules or any words that might cause someone to feel left out because of race, religion, or unstated circumstances. Whatever and whoever each of us understood God to be was in attendance that night. He/She had not been called to the event—but just showed up, happy to take part in the dance of humanity.

The crowd flowed out onto the cobblestone plaza, sat on benches, and talked in hushed reverence for what they had just shared. We gazed into a field of stars that were closer for us than they had ever been. "Happy Birthday Sharon" I said "Welcome to the magic of pilgrimage, Buen Camino."

"We are all made of Star Stuff." ~Carl Sagan

11

THE ROMAN ROAD

Wisdom is the principal thing:
Therefore get wisdom:
And with all thy getting:
Get understanding.
Proverbs, IV 7. (KJV)

I have surrendered to the camino and its teaching. Yesterday I disposed of a sorcerer and escaped his spell of fear—on this day I just wanted to be available for whatever showed up. Now that I had overcome the restraint of suffering and pain, my mind, senses, and perceptions became tuned and open.

Sometimes when I shook hands or hugged another pilgrim my mind would sense their pain, joy, or unhappiness. I was learning to respond with compassion and acceptance, and not judge what I saw or felt. A few have had an unconscious awareness of this insight and started talking about the burdens they bear. I can only give encouragement and positive reinforcement to dreams that are faltering. We each must defeat our own demons. I always encouraged the continuation of the quest—to welcome the confrontation, and know that there was bliss in victory.

Dr. Wayne Dyer said it best: "Instead of believing that you know what's best for others, trust that they know what's best for themselves."

I had decided that I would walk ten miles to Caldadilla de la Cueza where there would be little to discover but much to learn. Sharon was walking with me but planned to continue to Terradillos de losTemplarios or travel even further.

For reasons that I didn't understand, she had a self-imposed schedule that left her exhausted at day's end with little time to explore. She and others in similar situations would tell me that "I can't be gone two or three months, I need to get back." I never did understand why the limitations were so clearly scripted. Were they unworthy of staying longer?

I knew a retired woman in North Carolina who told me when I left for this trip, how much she envied my ability to travel. She said she had ". . . always wanted to see Europe and Greece." "Why don't you go?" I asked. "Oh, I could never leave my little dogs," she told me. Many of us choose to live in the purgatory of our past by installing walls of limitations to prevent our escape into the garden of an authentic life. The exciting news is that we always have a choice.

Late at night, when alone, we retreat to the attic of our minds. There, we carefully wrap and place our most cherished dreams in little boxes and tie them up tightly with attractive satin bows of emotions. Pinned to the outside in faded script are the instructions to "only open after I die."

A lot of today's path was on the old Calzada Romana or Roman Road. Over two thousand years of traffic and some parts still look really great. According to historical accounts, this large section of road traverses low, swampy land which required the builders to bring in over 100,000 tons of rock just to raise the surface above winter flood levels. We can only imagine the labor and architects required to build such expansive roads that have survived over two thousand years. No wonder, extensive Roman ruins and villas have been excavated nearby.

Caesar built this section of the Via Aquitaine to connect Burgos with Astorga. Then as now, the wheat fields were gold and were treated as such. I walked Caesar's road all day and saw only wheat, more golden and ready for harvest than any I had seen in all of Basque country, just a few weeks past. Occasionally there would be long lines of trees planted at angles to form windbreaks protecting the fragile stalks from powerful gusts that sporadically skipped across the plains.

We walked mostly in silence. Our only companions were the finches, sparrows and doves and on one occasion, a large foot-long lizard startled us as he ran across the dusty road. His lime green body sported a bright red chest and cone shaped eyes that turned to take in the full panorama. Midway across, he stopped and inflated his colorful chest like a balloon before launching back into the wheat fields. He was saying, "You can't catch me," I told Sharon.

I checked into the only albergue the small adobe town of Calzadilla de la Cueza had to offer. I was too happy with my new found body to push things. Besides, I had simple plans for laundry and an afternoon snooze on the patio. I walked Sharon the three blocks to the western edge of the village before stopping to take a remembrance photo and bidding a final "buen camino."

There were no shops, no restaurants, no bakery, and no "Tienda' for fruits and vegetables. There was a bar that managed to serve a strange hybrid food somewhere between American fast food and Spanish country. It did not taste like either. Like many remote locations on planet earth, food would have to be brought in frozen or under refrigeration. Fresh would not be an option here, and most of us understood. Some twenty-first century pilgrims may expect too much. In towns like Calzadilla, the rest of us are humbled with gratitude for what we do receive.

The next morning, I awoke feeling empowered to walk around the world and back by midday. "I must be careful not to become one of the fast crowds just because I can," I thought. A city of great mystery and historical significance lay only thirteen miles to the west. Sahagun's promise of legends to explore lightened my step and extended my stride into a day's journey that never lost its magic.

Terradillos de los Templarios is a small village that has no remains of the castles, churches or hospices built there as part of what was a thirteenth century stronghold for the Templars. Instead there were two modern albergues that traded on the fame of the name. The first, at the village entrance, proclaimed itself Albergue of the Templars—very much at odds with the modern motel-look-alike building it occupied.

It sat behind a fenced front yard with sprinklers working full force on the feeble grass lawn. Halfway through town, an older building proclaimed itself to be Albergue Jacques de Molay, with a large mural of the fourteenth century martyred Grand Master of the Templars painted on the side wall. Terradillos, the shadows were there, but the stories have long faded into the history books.

Moratinos welcomed me with a new modern albergue at the village entrance. A large sign out front proclaimed squash soup with ginger and sauerbraten as the day's special. It was too early for lunch but the kind German proprietors were happy to serve me the delicious cream soup on the front terrace. The tranquil sunbaked village held a charming surprise. What appeared to be rolling green hillsides across the camino path were actually dwellings, part straw and part mud, built similar to Hobbit houses. Grass and vegetation covered the entire rounded structures with doors and windows cut-in at street level. Chimneys and television antennas were the only indication that the structures were not small hills themselves. I wondered if such wise construction, using nature as an insulator against summer heat and frigid winters, could pass any of our modern city codes.

San Nicolas del Real Camino was the last village that I would pass in Palencia. The border to the Province of Leon was just a mile from there and the town of Sahagun would be on the near horizon. San Nicolas's warm adobe hospitality and charm had an intriguing early history with the Templars—who traded the town to King Alfonso VIII in 1183. It certainly deserved some time to enjoy a tapa of Serrano Ham and wine in the plaza.

The Provincia de Leon would provide a kaleidoscope of terrain, culture, and history during the coming weeks. It is the largest, most populous, and wealthiest province that the camino passes through. The flat, irrigated agricultural plain flows to the doorstep of the region's great capital city of Leon. West of the city, the Leon Mountains shelter remnants of the little—known Maragato culture. The isolation, mystery and abandoned villages fascinate and draw pilgrims into the obscure origins of these mysterious people—their food, dress and language. Before entering Galicia on the western border, Leon will show off its famed microclimate of vineyards and orchards, and Spain's second largest wine district, the Bierzo.

Through no planning of my own, destiny would have me arrive in Leon at the beginning of the city's largest annual celebration—the weeklong Festival of San Juan and San Pedro. My fellow pilgrims planned to walk through the city and stay well beyond its borders. We had been warned that celebrants from all over the region converge on Leon for the week. All lodging was booked for the event and pilgrim hostels would strictly enforce the standard rule of only one night of stay. I imagined that maybe, just maybe, the magic of the camino would find me an affordable pensión for a few days of celebration. Tonight I would be the guest of fabled Sahagun.

I arrived at the Albergue Cluny, housed on the second level of the ancient Iglesia de la Trinidad, only to find the twenty foot tall medieval doors locked. A local shopkeeper advised me to go to the side. There the wide stone steps lead to another great pair of medieval carved doors. I pushed on the giant brass handle; then I tried to shake them open. They were locked. My new friend who was watching my botched break-in yelled out to me from below, "Pull the rope." Hanging above my head was a very hefty rope that disappeared through a hole into the thick stone wall. I pulled very hard and a ton of wood creaked open. The first floor of the church housed the town tourist office, which operated on banker's hours. When they were at lunch, pilgrims would have to use the rope to enter the side doors.

The setting for my lodging that night could have been out of a grand opera. The second level had been dropped in across the entirety of the old church leaving the first floor as offices with ceilings at normal height. The remainder of the old building soared above the pilgrim's quarters for over fifty feet in majestic vaults forming cubicles for our bunks arranged in groups of six. The great leaded glass windows and stark brick and stone walls, shorn of gilt and adornment, left only the architecture to speak for its wonder.

Sahagun is a big city with a population of 170,000 but its history and soul remains inside the old walled historic center. Citizens gather, eat, drink and barter in cafés and bars within the confines of the Plaza Mayor and the Plaza Santiago. In addition to an early Roman presence, Saint Facundo and Saint Primitivo were martyred here in the fourth century. The name Sahagun is derived from San Facundo whose namesake monastery was one of the richest and most powerful in all Spain during the dark ages.

The city's rich history includes cycles of destruction and rebuilding by Romans, Visigoths, Muslims, Christians, knights and not a few kings. We can just imagine the endless cruelties and barbaric acts of war fostered on the many generations of innocent citizens who have suffered for the conquest of this little town. Perhaps the bricks of empire are forged from their blood and souls. In another two thousand years, who knows what will be fashioned from the bricks and mortar of our bones and DNA?

The sun rose strong the morning I left Sahagun onto flat plains with little opportunity for water or shade. After a hot day on the road alone, I walked into Calzada de los Hermanillos (Road of the Little Brothers), whose low slung buildings and hot dusty streets looked every bit like an Arizona desert town. Despite its small size there were two locations for pilgrims to stay, with a restaurant attached to one of them. Neither was open. The camino had split just outside Sahagun into the Old Roman Road, which ran north of the highway and the Pilgrim's Road, which was more direct. It was on one of the man-made sendas following the new highway. They would not connect again until Mansilla de las Mulas some twenty-two miles later. It was clear that the villages and experiences would be different but the deciding factor for me was that the Roman Road was away from highways and modern infrastructure.

Via Trajana, the town restaurant and hostel, sat on the path as I entered town. Two farmers on the patio were in animated discussion about some machinery parts to be delivered. They greeted me without looking up or slowing down from talking and drinking beer. Must not be part of the establishment, I thought, or questions would have been asked. No one else was around but when I looked through an open window to the kitchen, a matronly woman dressed in a full bodied apron was quick to offer service. Soon I was enjoying an excellent breakfast.

Talking With Cats

The Municipal Albergue is in the town's former school house. It has twenty beds with four bunks to each cubicle. Janie, an attractive red-haired woman from New Zealand was the only bunk mate in my cubicle. Nearby was a young couple from Australia and an assortment of Germans, Swiss and French to complete that night's attendance at sixteen. Miguel was our only host in the little place but no other was needed. He hand-painted the Cross of Santiago on small shells and gave them to anyone who did not have one. He was a one-man show making our new home a haven of hospitality.

The heat was the main topic of discussion—primarily how to avoid the worst of it. The little group started making plans to leave early around four or five a.m. at the latest. They decided to walk twenty-six miles the next day in order to arrive in Leon. My modest goal of twelve miles to Mansilla de las Mulas would get me there by noon at the latest. Too much good food, wine and history to enjoy—If I rush the teacher will not come. That night I heard the familiar clicks of trekking poles on cobblestones at eleven. Two pilgrims were passing through town— walking the moonlit camino—under the Milky Way.

Here I am—drunk again—on life, on Spain, on this whole experience of pilgrimage. I left Little Brothers at 6:45 after having breakfast with Miguel. The day's walk was pleasant with most of it on the actual old Roman Road. Portions of it were covered with new sand topping, though on the steeper grades, rains had eroded it down to the old stone bed. At one point there were long rectangular mounds near the road, which were enclosed with fencing. I could only guess that they might contain the remains of a Roman village.

I came across a young priest from New York who had slowed his pace to inspect side paths which might lead south to join the main camino running near the highway. We agreed that the best option would be to continue on until the village of Reliegos where the crossover would be more clearly marked. We had experiences to share, and with neither being in a hurry, the companionship was welcome. Though this was a well-marked dirt path, no one had passed us all morning. Others were well ahead of us, having struck out at five a.m. or they were on the faster straight road along the highway.

Father James had come to the camino to reconnect with his faith and build a deeper relationship with God. He had been challenged with the pace and rigidity of the world "out there" and needed to find his own stillness. I was surprised to hear him speak about the many daily challenges of tolerance and acceptance of fellow pilgrims. "I thought that I was the only one here to learn that lesson," I joked.

He told me about a group of recent college grads that he met in Burgos. "I had been walking with two, thirty-year-old professionals and was invited to join them for a beer. They were part of a larger group who had initiated 'A Camino Pub Crawl.' Every day they got up early, walked twenty to thirty miles and drank all evening until lock-out," he told me. "The challenge was to see how drunk and wasted they could get and still get up early and walk the next day."

The camino brings all personalities and afflictions of our modern times to its portals. It is no different here than in a big city; the path offers it's teaching to all people, all religions, all nationalities and to all economic backgrounds. Father James spoke about the true teaching of love, acceptance and non-judgment: "We cannot judge the 'pub crawlers' or the 'fast-crowd' for not listening to the teachings along the way—that is putting ourselves in an exalted position of knowing and being better than them."

If others on the camino are able to disturb our search for self then we are not very secure in accepting who we are. Often, what we judge in others is simply a projection of what we don't like in ourselves. Father James and I agreed that we would see many strange behaviors while walking the camino but it was their journey. Something brought them here—let them find it. No one has to choose to be with others whose habits and words are disturbing but we can make the choice not to judge them. Be still within our own truth and let it grow.

Famished after the long hot walk to Mansilla de las Mulas, I hurried through a cold shower at the Amigos del Camino Municipal Hostel and went in search of lunch. Four weeks in Spain had taught me that the big meal of the day is served in most cities from one until four p.m., which is a perfect schedule for my body. In the evening fresh fruit and tea makes for a restful sleep.

Talking With Cats

Restaurants put out a sandwich board listing the choices for the *comida del dia* (meal of the day) and the price. It always includes three courses with three to four selections for each course. Wine and water are included and in many locations they will be brought when you are seated (only tourists choose white wine, I was told by one server.) Once you find the menu that meets your needs, you step inside to a bar with a few small tables. There will be a bartender, maybe two or three patrons drinking wine or beer, but no one dining. Often the bartender does not greet you; he assumes that you know where to go, since; after all it's time for the midday meal.

Such was the case in Mansilla de las Mulas. I walked through the bar to the back where two sets of doors were paneled with frosted glass. One set of doors bore two silhouettes, one of a lady in formal Spanish dress and the other a gentleman. The other doors were plain with small brass letters running vertical on the frame that said 'Comedor' (dining room). There was no hostess, one of the busy servers waved me to a table. A full bottle of fine red Bierzo wine and a liter of spring water appeared instantly (had I been expected?).

The room held about twelve tables of varying sizes all set with white linen, napkins, and stemmed water and wine glasses. A group of ten locals seated near the far wall were receiving bread and placing their order. Typically, there are no menus unless it is an à la carte or tourist fine-dining restaurant. The server recites the first course choices and waits on everyone to choose before going to the second (entrée) selections. Another table of three, next to mine, had received their first course. It looked promising.

I choose a regional specialty to start; tureen of seafood soup in saffron broth, to be followed with albondigas con pimento (Spanish meat balls braised with local red peppers and potatoes.) I was presented with a crisp baguette, an empty bowl, a ladle, and a large tureen of rich broth and seafood which was left on the table. I could serve myself as much as I wanted. A local family of six arrived and was to be seated to the rear of the room requiring them to pass in front of my table. "Buen probecho" (Bon appetite) they each greeted me with a slight bow and a smile as they filed by.

In Spain no one enters a room where others are dining without wishing them the traditional greeting. Conversations at the new table revealed them to be local ranchers and the formality accorded the distinguished "Don Eduardo" (Lord Edward) may have been more than just respect. Many Spanish families continue using their noble titles; often with a heraldic crest carved in the stone lintels over the entry to their estates. It is not unusual for some of the crests and names to go back to the sixteenth or even the twelfth century.

By three p.m. all the tables were full; each newcomer greeted my table as though I too, had a crest carved in stone. Albondigas in Spain are as unique to its cuisine as Swedish meat balls are to Stockholm. They are a great comfort food and these were among the best. I soon discovered that I had finished the entire bottle of wine. Another tradition, even though I was alone, a full bottle had been brought to my table. The charge was the same whether I drank one glass or the whole bottle. Earlier on the Camino, at another restaurant, I had asked the server, "Can I have a half bottle or just a glass?" She looked at me in amazement as though I could not arrive at the logical conclusion alone, "Just drink what you want—you don't have to finish it," she advised.

Natilla, (boiled custard with cinnamon) and an espresso coffee completed a sublime excursion into traditional Spanish cooking. I must add that the above meal cost only ten Euros. Few countries with the sophistication of Spanish culinary heritage can produce such a fine bargain.

Part Two
The Awakening

Above all, do not lose your desire to walk:
Every day I walk myself into a state of well-being
and walk away from every illness.
I have walked myself into my best thoughts.
~ Søren Kierkegaard

12

FESTIVAL IN LEON

The time has come to set out for the sacred ground—the mountain, the temple, the ancestral home—that will stir our heart and restore our sense of wonder. It is down the path to the deeply real where time stops and we are seized by the mysteries. This is the journey that we cannot, not take.
~Phil Cousineau, the Art of Pilgrimage

"Remember Burgos!" my feet and legs cried out as I began to walk on concrete into another great city on the Camino de Santiago. Leon was founded by the Romans in the year seventy B.C.E. to protect their gold mines in Galicia and it soon became the Roman capital of northern Iberia. I carried two maps of Leon's city plan—still functioning as the Romans designed it. Principal streets were laid out north-south and east-west within a walled city whose entrances were four grand gates—portals that announced to all "We are a great and rich city! Respect us!" Evidently protection was not the gates strongpoint as every invading horde that swept across the Iberian plains in the dark ages and into medieval times took the city—destroying and rebuilding it. Today, no Roman buildings remain—parts of the wall and baths under the cathedral are all that's left to tell their story.

The pilgrim's road from Mansilla de las Mulas to Leon runs parallel to or in places actually on the side of the busy highway N-601. As in Burgos most of the day's path would be on punishing concrete. When I arrived in Villarente that little internal voice was shouting "Suffering is optional." "Ah yes, so it is," I replied, while boarding a city bus that headed into Leon. The central bus station sits next to RENFE train station on the south side of the River Bernesga. Modern commercial and industrial Leon surrounds the two transportation hubs and is merely functional and utilitarian at best—that changed at the river.

The grand Palencia Avenue Bridge led directly to the old city's heart. The town was in full festival mode with trucks and city utilities installing the final touches for San Juan-San Pedro Week. The Casa de los Botines (built 1892-1893) is the modernist neo-Gothic palace designed by Barcelona's famed architect, Antonio Gaudi. The four-story palace stands overlooking the expansive plaza where trucks with cranes were unloading heroic sized floral topiaries—each constructed from hundreds of potted blooming plants.

Across the Plaza San Marcelo, a stage had been erected where groups of school children, regional dance troupes and music ensembles were taking turns at rehearsal. Costumed performers, young and old alike, flitted through the crowd of tourists and pilgrims. The gay circus atmosphere was not unlike being on a giant rehearsal stage for the Opera Carmen.

An arched arcade ran the length of one side of the plaza where giant costumed puppets were being laid out in the passageway. I stopped at the adjacent city tourist information office for a schedule of events and to learn about the huge puppets.

'Gigantes Y Cabezudos' (giants and bigheads) have been a tradition at Spanish festivals since medieval times to depict the stories of leaders, invaders and the common folk—often in a satirical manner. Here the giants were twelve-foot-tall paper mache figures of Moors, kings, popes, and folk heroes. They were elaborately costumed over an intricate framework, with strong, athletic young men strapped inside so they could animate the giants in a street parade. Small view screens had been sown in the costumes at eye level to help the animators find their way. They were followed by the 'big heads'—three foot tall heads that were worn over the head and upper torso of costumed individuals—portraying both mythical and town tradesmen. Two red-sashed pied-pipers led the procession.

Feeling inspired by the excitement, I inquired if any reasonable lodging could be found within the old city walls. The tourist office maintained a computer update of every hostel, pension, and hotel room that became available.

"What is your price range?" the receptionist inquired.

"Twenty to thirty Euros is the maximum I can afford," I told her. Leon is a big city with big city prices and here was this old man looking for village prices during a major sold-out festival. Silence reigned behind the counter as the three clerks turned to look at each other, trying to conceal their shock or sympathy for my plight.

"The city and suburbs are completely sold out throughout the festival. Even private homes have rented their extra bedrooms," one clerk said apologetically. She picked up the desk telephone and dialed a number. "There is a pension that expects a vacancy soon, but they could not give us a date. Please wait I am calling her."

A hushed conversation continued on the phone—the tone of an exchange we might hear used at a funeral or in a hospital during last rites. She turned to me, "She has a room that will be ready soon. She will rent it to you for twenty Euros . . . how many days do you want?"

"Five," I told her.

The elegant elderly lady who greeted me at the Pension Oviedo gave me three keys: one to the building proper, one to the third floor, and one for my room. My new home was well appointed with crisp linen and a tiled bathroom hosting an antique porcelain tub. I bathed thinking of the magical journey that had begun manifesting everything I could imagine. I was about to begin five days of celebration and pageantry in a city with over two thousand years of history and architecture to explore.

The majestic Gothic Cathedral dates from the thirteenth century and is the fourth to be built on the same spot. This one is said to be a copy of the Rheims Cathedral. City brochures proclaim it as "The Cathedral without Walls" referring to the multiple storied tiers of stain glass windows. Leon is reputed to have more glass and less stone than any other cathedral in Spain. Over the course of several visits, it was dazzling to watch the play of sunlight as it passed over the windows from sunrise to sunset. Nothing in all Christendom is more inspiring than to stand in the nave of Leon's Cathedral, when the shafts of sunlight stream through the rose window and fall into shimmering jewels of pulsating light, far below.

The windows portray a variety of scenes, many outside the normal sacred pantheon of church art. There are hunting scenes and vignettes of medieval life, floral gardens and courtly life. The intensity of the jewel-like color in the windows is living testimony to the craftsmanship that existed in what was then the most time-intensive and expensive portion of church building. The mastery of encasing large walls of glass in delicate filigreed stone defies conventional wisdom of architecture. During medieval times, it was considered the work of God.

That evening I walked the wide tree-lined promenade that bordered the river. On the opposite shore the festival's nightly attraction for the masses was ablaze with lights and music. The Ferria (Fair) of San Juan-San Pedro was an international exposition of Latin food and culture. The line of tents culminated in a carnival and circus that stretched another two miles along the river, neon lighted ferris wheels and fantasy rides mirrored in its waters.

Sweepers and cleaning crews were on the cobblestone streets at daybreak—scrubbing and vacuuming the old town into a respectable welcome for the day's revelers. I sat at the corner café having breakfast and watching preparations while few others stirred. I looked over the calendar of cultural events scheduled for the week. That night a concert of classical music featuring a renowned ensemble would play at the cultural center and the opera, Madame Butterfly, was scheduled for the following night. I waited for advance tickets at the music store, hoping to attend both events.

In order to stay at pilgrim hostels and to receive a *Compostela,* (*a* Certificate of Completion from the cathedral in Santiago), it is necessary to carry an official pilgrim's passport or *credencial*. Each hostel must stamp the credencial and enter your passport number and name into their official log book. It is necessary to provide proof that you walked at least the last one hundred kilometers on arrival in Santiago. Those on bicycles must have stamps of proof for the last two hundred kilometers. Churches, museums, restaurants and bars along the Camino also have official stamps to recognize attendance.

I had walked only one third the daily average distance of most pilgrims, therefore, I had more hostels and time for stamps from historic locations and churches. The fifty-six spaces in my pilgrims' passport were almost filled, yet I had only completed half the journey. The Association of Friends of the Camino de Santiago maintains an office near the Plaza San Marcelo where I was able to receive a credencial insert.

Many cities along the camino can boast of the art and treasures in their churches and museums but perhaps none can equal that of Leon's Royal Basilica of Saint Isodoro. True, the three great cathedrals along the camino contain walls of stained glass windows, church size chapels, organs and sculpture that dwarf St. Isodoro but they do not equal the collective of this masterpiece.

San Isodoro's treasury and museum are crammed with enough high quality art to rival that of any major city. The Romanesque murals in the crypt are considered to be the finest in Spain if not in all Europe. Spain has hosted waves of divergent cultures during the past two thousand years. Like many great civilization, the conquerors built their empires atop the most prominent ruins of the vanquished. St. Isodoro stands on the site of a medieval monastery dedicated to John the Baptist, which was constructed on the ruins of a Roman temple to Mercury.

The basilica was built in the eleventh century by the great warrior King Fernando I of Castile and Leon. His relentless battles brought the Moors to seek peace. Unable to pay the kings demands in gold they offered instead the relics of martyrs and art that had been plundered from Andalusia's cities. The horde of Christian relics was of little use to the Moors, but along with the bones of St. Isodoro, the collection was a treasure trove for Castile and Leon. The king created a commission to build the basilica which was completed in just eleven years.

My intention in supplying a brief description of St. Isodoro's Basilica, or any other landmark mentioned in the book is to illustrate that wherever you may walk or take pilgrimage, there is history that will enlighten and enhance your journey. Like the camino, I prefer to build anticipation and excitement well in advance of departure on any journey—books and films are a good way to start. Once we are informed, nothing beats being there—as we imagine touching, feeling, seeing and sensing the ghosts and spirits of each place. When standing at great battle sites, ruins or majestic cathedrals we should not shake our heads in judgment—but in awe. Like it or not, those are the shoulders of history that we stand on. There is great wisdom to learn from the bones of the past.

Northern Spain alone has hosted three great cultures that predate modern Christian times and remain vital today. The Camino de Santiago passes through two of them. The Basque of the northeast and the Celts of Galicia in the northwest can fill a library by themselves. Then add the Romans, the Dark Ages, Visigoths, Charlemagne, and the Moorish occupation just to arrive at the year one thousand.

In the past millennium, the crusades and warring kingdoms of Leon, Castile, Asturias, Navarra, Portugal, and Aragon have defeated, destroyed, defended and rebuilt their empires many times. It was only in 1492 that Fernando and Isabel defeated the Moors at Granada, to unite Spain for the first time. All of this and the many civil wars of the nineteenth and early twentieth century left much of empire and the ages of knights and kings in ruins.

Many of my fellow pilgrims regretted that their preparation had been limited to reading just one of the Camino guidebooks and possibly seeing a few travel films on its major cities. The pilgrimage is not just a road that leads to the city of Santiago and its saint—it is a whole universe of discovery and the treasures of many kingdoms and cultures along the way. Please check the bibliography for some reads that inspired and informed my journey.

In the heart of Leon, just off the Plaza Regla that fans out from the majestic cathedral, I found one of the best restaurants to date. Las Termas is housed in the Hostal Albany with service at a row of tables on a narrow pedestrian street. My first course that afternoon was a delicate eggplant and veal lasagna with béchamel sauce. The second course of braised osso buco of pork, demi-glace with patatas bravas (a crispy Spanish spicy potato) was braised to tender perfection. The house red wine was a fine reserve from Bierzo and the house dessert was a perfect tiramisu. I managed to have two more meals at Las Termas before leaving Leon.

All bunks at albergues on the camino are supplied with a clean bottom sheet and pillow case. No covering or towels are provided. For that reason everyone must carry a light sleeping bag or sleep-sack. I had a silk sleep-sack which turned out to be perfect for summer but would not have been adequate for early spring or fall. It was so comfortable that I had grown quite fond of my 'little blanky' just in time to lose it in one of the villages. Perhaps while packing in haste one morning it rolled under my bunk—regardless, it was not in my backpack when I prepared for bed that night. Leon would have outfitters for a new one.

I learned from my friends at the tourist information booth the location for a sports outfitter on Calle Rua. I knew that the cold, rainy mountains of Galicia would require a sleeping bag and Armeria Castro had the largest selection in Leon. Roberto, the friendly clerk at the shop became a friend and a good resource for a sleeping bag, local tales and family history in Leon. "Yes," he told me that "the area was suffering from unemployment and the nation's financial hardships but not as much as towns off the camino. I am very grateful to be employed. I have friends who have been looking for work for many months—it's tough."

Roberto asked me if I were going to attend the festival's two bullfights. He explained, "One will be from horseback in the medieval old style and the other will be traditional with the matador on foot." I told him that I would consider attending because I wanted to better understand the emotions and traditions of the custom and of the Spanish people.

"Most foreigners, especially Americans, are very disturbed by this custom," Roberto said.

"To many of us it is barbaric and akin to turning bears against bulls in the Roman Coliseum," I told him.

"Yes, I took a young American couple to the fights a few years ago. She fainted and they had to leave during the first fight," he said.

"Some cultural traditions are very difficult to accept when they are outside our experience," I said.

The Sonor Ensemble consisted of ten members selected from leading orchestras and chamber groups in Spain. That evening's program included the world premiere of a new composition by Jose Luis Turina. The remainder of the evening's program included popular works by Bartok, Ligeti, Kodaly, and as a finale, El Amour Brujo by Manuel de Falla. I left the concert hall and stepped out into a city of complete bedlam and chaos.

Traffic had come to a standstill—those who remained in their cars were leaning on their horns nonstop. Thousands, maybe hundreds of thousands, were in the streets hugging, shouting, drinking and making noise any way possible. Spain had just won a game during the Euro World Cup Soccer match that would send them to the championship. Seldom had I seen such intense patriotism. Fans were dressed in red and gold—the team colors, while others were wrapped in the Spanish flag. It took me an hour to push through the screaming celebration and arrive the few blocks back at my pension. Police were everywhere, but they were patient with the crowd and polite to everyone. Their only concern was for the safety of property and individuals like me. "Are you okay sir?" one asked as I tried to push through a crowd at my street corner.

I went to bed with my window open—the explosion of fireworks, horns, shouting and the discordant music of drunken impromptu bands reverberating off the walls like missiles. But I didn't go to sleep, at least not for a long time. The excitement was contagious—the kid in me really wanted to go join the throng of revelers. Just lay still and let the vibrations continue to wash over my imagination and the dreams to come, I told myself. It was 1:30 in the morning.

Sometimes, to get to know a place, a country or a people, you just have to sit, watch, smell and be very observant. It is sort of like watching a movie; either catch all the details or miss the set-up for the next scene. In life there is no fast forward or rewind—catch it now or lose it. And so it was that day. I sat on a bench facing the cathedral, totally entranced in the moment, with life in the Spanish city of Leon on Thursday, June 28, 2012.

I was the director, cameraman and crew and at that moment, mentally filming a wedding. The cathedral is a major focus of life in Leon and it doesn't close or, at least, it is not supposed to close. Today, there was more conflict than resolution as Spanish society assembled for what appeared to be a nuptial union of the elite. The great nave and choir stall filled with well-coiffed wedding guests while the everyday business of mass continued in one of the immense side chapels.

The city's poor, the elderly and the tradesfolk had to walk down a passageway behind a twenty-foot-tall ornate iron grillwork to get to the chapel for mass. The bride, wearing a long-flowing-bejeweled lace train, the beautiful attendants, the elegant children as ring bearers and the couture dressed guests were just too much not to watch. No one made it to mass. Instead, the motley crew all lined up behind the grill work to gawk at the proceedings. I am sure when seen from the wedding party we looked like a bunch of ill-mannered prisoners behind bars. The bride and groom became nervous, shooting fearful side-glances as they knelt on the velvet cushions at the altar. The mighty organ trumpeted a call to God but the growing crowd behind the grill just jockeyed for better positions—we only had eyes for the young couple and the elegant ceremony.

The bishop and the bride's father became involved in some complicated hand signals which soon had the church steward trying to move the uninvited crowd away. Parishioners railed at him that the church was public and that they had every right to attend mass. Most of the tourists were compliant but the elderly locals put up quite a protest. A few seniors enjoyed running around the steward in the great hall since it was one man against the many. When he retreated to bring out one stray, another would dash by him. Finally, the last defiant elder was herded through the great doors as the flustered steward followed her and closed them with a loud bang and a padlock. Just outside the cathedral gates sat an antique Rolls-Royce touring car with chauffeur in full livery, standing at attention.

Soon after the big wedding experience, I shared the story with Roberto at his shop.

"We are not like the Spanish of the south. Leon was settled by the Romans—we are Roman people," he declared. "The roads are Roman, the ruins are Roman, the foods we eat comes from the Roman table—our blood is not Spanish; it is Roman." He continued; "Many people think we are a country of Flamencos—the so-called Spanish guitar, gypsies and bullfights. The people of the south embody the modern myths of our culture. They also retain much of the Moorish blood."

I told him that the same is true in America; that we also have many cultures with distinct bloodlines, foods and manners of speech.

"I am sure that you discovered the same pride in the Catalan and Basque people when you were there and you will find the same when you get to Galicia. The culture that most people think of as Spanish is unique to southern Spain. We in the north are much more diverse than that," he concluded.

The opera that night started at 9:30. Madame Butterfly utilized the Leon Symphonic Orchestra and a fine display of regional voices—some of them exceptional. It was interesting to be a native English speaker, watching an opera set in Japan, being sung in Italian, with Spanish super-titles. The production had been mounted exclusively for one night at the festival; as a result the sets were not remarkable. The evening however, was a musical triumph.

The final curtain came down at 12:30 in the morning and I stepped out into a city as alive as though it were lunch time. The elderly were strolling about arm-in-arm; children were playing, buying balloons and sweet treats while cafes and bars attracted a standing only crowd. I found a single chair at a sidewalk café where servers were rushing to and fro with trays of fresh hot churros and chocolate. At another place and another time in my life I might have felt that it was too late to be out celebrating—but that was then and this was now. That night, I just knew that the smiling crescent moon was meant for me.

An eerie silence hung over the city of Leon the next morning—wisps of fog came over from the river and crept down the chilly streets. There were no cafés or bars open. Even the small café where I breakfasted every morning was closed; its chairs stacked against the wall and secured with chains. Worse still, its competitors were closed too. There was no traffic, not one car came by where I stood, normally a very busy intersection near my pensión.

Sure, it was San Pedro Saints Day, but I did not know that the city would close completely. Surely someplace would open for coffee. In contrast to the late night celebrations that I had witnessed just seven hours before, this was like being in a surrealistic dream-scape. In search of a tall café-con-leche I started walking down the wide avenue toward the cathedral and Plaza San Marcelo. A yellow street sweeper, brushes spinning, turned the corner and headed in my direction. A few blocks further a crew of sanitation workers was blasting grime from the sidewalks—dragging heavy fire hoses as though they were extension cords. A lone police car sat astride the center divider, mid-avenue, the officers sipping on coffee and chatting as the city prepared itself for another day of celebration.

Near the cathedral, a café had opened for breakfast with inside service only. I could see that the place was packed and the counter was filled with platters of fresh croissants and hot sugar coated churros. I stepped inside to the heady aroma of coffee, hot chocolate, steamed milk and the unmistakable essence of sugar and cinnamon as it was dusted onto hot fried pastry. Outside, all cafés and bars had stacked their tables and chairs against the walls or taken them inside to make room for the sanitation crew—obviously, the merchants knew the routine.

In order for pilgrims to navigate through large cities, the camino is marked with brass scallop shells embedded in the sidewalks. As in medieval times, pilgrim's paths are directed to pass all churches, monasteries, convents and hospices where they can both offer devotion and receive shelter and blessings for the journey ahead. In small villages the path enters from the east and passes straight through town where all services are centered on the Plaza Major. The camino in Leon, as in other larger cities, follows the winding route of its historic sacred landmarks.

I found a brass shell in front of the cathedral and set out to follow its trail through the town. Sunday morning, when I would return to the camino, there would not be an opportunity to explore the many adventures on its path. Even more importantly, I could find where to pick up the road close to my pensión.

It was an adventure. At one place, in a narrow cobblestone alleyway, there was a small poster for an art show. El Mundo Del Alexandro Maximus (The World of Alexander the Great) was an exhibit in a museum on the back side of the Basilica de San Isodoro. Nowhere else was this exhibit mentioned—not in the extensive booklet issued by the city for the festival, not in the museum guide available at the tourist office, nor in the guides provided at San Isodoro.

The exhibit was not extensive but certainly it helped fill in some details missing from other grander exhibits that I knew from Athens and London. The museum also had an interesting collection of early religious art, which included Jewish, Islamic, Coptic, Egyptian and Christian pieces.

The camino completes its path around the plaza of San Isodoro and heads down the broad Avenue Quiñones to one of the grandest palaces on the entire pilgrimage. San Marcos is described in one historical account as the Mother of all Motherhouses. The original medieval structure suffered structural damage and was demolished early in the sixteenth century.

The construction for the current building was commissioned by King Fernando in 1514 and took two hundred years to complete. The palace is a masterpiece of Renaissance Plateresque architecture built on a heroic scale beautifully balanced on the back side of the park-like Plaza San Marcos. The church of San Marcos was built in similar style and is attached to the palace on the right side. The palace and grounds are bordered on the left by the Bernesga River where the ornate San Marcos Bridge would take me west early Sunday morning.

The building housed the Knights of the Order of Santiago and remained their seat of power throughout the middle ages. After the expulsion of the Moors, the Knights ceased being a military order, becoming an honorary one—as they remain today. The palace functioned as a monastery until 1837—followed by a series of transitions, when the Spanish government rescued it in 1961.

The Parador San Marcos is one of the most super luxurious hotels in the world. The building and grounds along with the church and attached museum offer patrons the grandest setting in the restored splendor of Renaissance Spain. Most folk are too intimidated to enter but the gracious staff is welcoming. In the lobby and reception room, tourists can stare in awe at one of the best preserved Mudejar-style coffered ceilings in the world. The museum is directly off the lobby and encircles the cloisters and church.

It would take a month's worth of my budget on the camino to stay one night at the Parador San Marcos but I could afford a meal in the dining room. For me, picking one meal at the Parador was like a death row prisoner having to choose his last supper before execution. Fortunately, the chef had anticipated my situation and created a selection he called The Gastronomy of Spain Tasting Menu.

The opening course consisted of Black Label Serrano ham, cold poached mountain trout with roasted peppers and aged goat cheese with tomato jam. The second course was also a trio of exquisite perfection with grilled octopus, country pate, and a poached egg presented in veal broth. Buttered bread crumbs were served to absorb the liquid goodness. The third course was a brochette of veal tenderloin in a wild mushroom reduction with roasted vegetables and steamed potato. Each of the above was paired with an appropriate regional wine. The fourth and final course was a many layered chocolate torte with brandy-marinated Spanish cherries. I lingered for a long time, sipping an espresso in the Palace of the Knights of Santiago.

Spain didn't invent bull fighting—they inherited it. The concept of killing the sacred bull follows an ancient thread from Mesopotamia, to Greece and India. The killing of the sacred bull is central to the cult of Mithros and its great symbols cover the palace at Knossos. Minoan wall murals depict scenes of 'bull leaping' where young athletes met the charging bull by grabbing his horns and vaulting across its back. For ancient astronomers and todays astrologers, the same sacred bull lives in the constellation Taurus.

Modern Spain has struggled with continuing the tradition of bull fighting as condemnation has rained down on them from countries, societies and animal rights groups far and wide. Spaniards themselves are divided in opinion over this controversy but traditions die hard as if the DNA from millennia of ceremony becomes activated every time they walk into a Plaza de Toros. Today's event was not to be the classic on foot Corrida with Matador. Rather it would be fought from horseback, a tradition inherited from antiquity through Portugal.

A Corrida de Rejones requires skilled horsemanship and that day's sell-out crowd had come to see Pablo Hermoso de Mendoza, one of Spain's finest mounted matadors. There were two others, both younger godsons to Hermoso's tutelage. When I closed my eyes, the crowd sounded very much like what I have experienced at an American football game (or European soccer match.) But it wasn't. Each fight opens with a demonstration in the art of horsemanship, a ceremony of grace and beauty achieved as rider and horse become one. The fight that follows is divided into three stages. A different horse is used in each stage, sometimes more. Matadors such as Hermoso may travel with as many as ten fine Arabian horses—bred and trained for these events.

All six bulls were killed that day but their deaths were quick and efficient, nothing compared to what I have seen in American slaughterhouses. I am in no way defending the tradition but if we are to be objective civil humans, part of that assumes our capacity for rational unemotional reasoning. Personally, I left the bullring with thoughts on how evolution has not cleansed us from barbaric acts, ritual cruelty and techniques of warfare.

I walked back into town along the river promenade—the carnival atmosphere on the other side floated across in aromas of charcoal cooked foods and a montage of sounds from the many bands mingled with screams from death-defying thrill rides. The city's population of 130,000 had expanded beyond its walls as the celebration of San Pedro danced on into the night. New pyramids of blooms had been added throughout the town, streets were scrubbed, and people were animated with joy and happiness. Leon looked like a great place to live. From where I stood, no one would have guessed the dire global headlines: Spain suffers 25 percent unemployment!

I spent my last day in Leon visiting the cathedral, listening to its great organ, meditating, being quiet and absorbing the pageant of history that had left so many fingerprints and so much evidence of its presence. I knew that with time, many medieval secrets could be coaxed out of the shadows to reveal their stories. That night I would attend a celebration of one of those stories. Set In the great Romanesque cloisters of San Isodoro, it had been 824 years in the making.

I returned to Las Termas for a final leisurely meal of salad, leek and potato soup and flan. The afternoon was filtered with soft rays of sunlight; there were fewer frames per second in every scene my mind filmed—sometimes I used stop-motion to observe a pigeon lifting in flight—jewel tones of throat feathers frozen in time. The melancholy music from a street musician on the plaza became my soundtrack—his violin telling stories he could never speak.

An elderly, ashen-faced woman slowly passed my table and made her way across the great plaza to the cathedral. Her opaque stockings sagged in places and had seams running up the back; she wore a black skirt and blouse, and carried a few stems of white roses wrapped in plain paper. Her black shoes were scuffed but they had sturdy heels and laced across the instep. Grey hair poked out of a black scarf whose fringe was mostly worn away. She didn't see me, she didn't see anyone, she didn't hear the music; she was silently rehearsing the prayer for departed souls. I watched her so intently that I felt like I had invaded her privacy.

The small posted announcement for that evening said there would be a concert of medieval music celebrating the government of Leon. It was to be held in the cloisters of San Isodoro which are off limits to all tours. If for no other reason, I intended to go. The concert was announced for 10:00 p.m. with no indication of ticket requirements or charge. Late that afternoon I went to the basilica to check things out. They were locked and closed. I found a policeman and explained the announcement, perhaps I had the date wrong or there was another cloister linked to the church. "No, the location is correct but the entrance is on the back street behind the complex," he told me, "and, sir, this is a proud and important event for all of Leon."

Regardless of how important the concert was to be, I only had hiking clothes to wear and the temperature was dropping rapidly—the old wrinkled windbreaker would have to do. I couldn't go out in the cold with a shaved head, so the wide, floppy brimmed cotton hat also had to be worn. Scuffed hiking boots completed an ensemble well suited to the homeless. Music fans come in many stripes and colors, tonight its REI chic, I told myself.

The first example of modern parliamentarianism in the history of Western Europe occurred here in 1188 with the Spanish Parliament of the Kingdom of Leon. The kingdom of King Alfonso's IX was under attack from its neighbors so he decided to summon the Royal Curia. Normally, the Curia only consisted of aristocrats, nobles, and bishops but the situation was so serious the king called for representatives of the urban middle class to be assembled with the Lords and Bishops.

For the first time since Ancient Greece a government was convened to represent all the people. John Adams had studied the Fuero of Leon and used its judicial model as a working manuscript when the founding fathers shaped the American Constitution. Just like the year 1188, that night in the cloisters of the Basilica of San Isodoro, the lords, bishops and people of Leon came together to celebrate their heritage.

I entered the great cloisters at 9:45 and grabbed one of the few remaining seats of the three hundred that filled the central plaza. An arched arcade with graceful columns surrounded all four sides and supported a second level. From the upper level hung many regal banners bearing the great seals and crests of Leon, the bishop, and the nobles. The crests were ancient ornate tapestries of velvets, gold bullion and embroidery suspended from medieval hardware. Under the arcade, the basilica's own treasure trove of stone sculptures, sarcophagi, urns, columns and capitals were strewn about as though the ruins of an empire had been assembled for the occasion.

The chairs were arrayed to face a stage that held a thirty piece wind ensemble, costumed in ceremonial military uniforms. The seated guests were in dark suits and evening clothes but the first few rows were still empty, having been reserved with ribbons. That soon changed as the bishops and a formally attired procession of reigning lords, ladies and knights of various orders including Santiago, were seated. Each wore great capes and the jeweled collars of office and rank. Had a satellite passed over Leon that night, it would have been easy to pick this humble pilgrim out in that illustrious audience. The arcade also held a large crowd of standing room only guests. There were a few speeches and an emotional moment when the audience stood to sing The Hymn of Leon.

The orchestra was a fine professional group and would have impressed the critics of any country. During the period that I understood to be an intermission, instead became a hushed enactment of fine dance theater. Gossamer clad young ladies formed a solemn procession down the center aisle. They each held a candle and moved to the music from a hypnotic medieval flute, until they arrived on stage. There, the whole flowed into a well-choreographed ballet.

Leon had presented me with the finest of hospitality and an opportunity to know its people, its history and rich culture. I was so bathed in joy that when I returned well after midnight, sleep was not necessary, I was already in a dream.

13

COMPANIONS

Many people die with their music still in them.
Why is this so?
Too often it is because they are always getting ready to live.
Before they know it, time runs out.
~Oliver Wendell Holmes

The next fourteen miles of camino out of Leon rose to a path that traveled on two very large mesetas. The small village of La Virgen Del Camino was the last settlement until Villar de Mazarife. Pilgrims were strung out on the road and many, like me, had slowed down to enjoy the tranquility and peace of the journey.

Abel, from South Korea, was the first to walk with me that day. Pilgrims develop a bond of acceptance and trust of each other which facilitates conversations to develop quickly about the most esoteric, political, and religious topics. Abel and I jumped into questions about our governments and their position on the world stage. I was curious about life in South Korea and how the constant threat of war from just across the border shaped their daily dialogue. More importantly I wanted to know how the college age youth, his age, saw their future?

Abel did not see himself isolated in a divided nation in Southeast Asia. He was a bio-tech grad student, who saw his future unfolding on the global stage. To him, Korea's division would heal in time. The threat of war was not a point to focus on,

"To be fixated on an enemy would be detrimental to the development of my country and its burgeoning industry," he told me.

I felt reassured for the world that fine young people like Abel would soon be in leadership positions. A new paradigm of possibilities was unfolding for their future.

Isaac Asimov once said, "Since we are drowning in an ocean of information, the most precious commodity in modern society is wisdom. Without wisdom and insight, we are left to drift aimlessly and without purpose, with an empty, hollow feeling after the novelty of unlimited information wears off." Wisdom can only come when political parties, nations and religions sit down to reasoned and informed democratic debate. The words and dogma of obsolete constitutions, religious doctrines and royal decrees will not guide us into a digital universe of quantum physics and the mysteries of the cosmos. The results of not accepting the wisdom of who we are becoming could be catastrophic.

We cannot continue the primal reaction of demonizing those we do not understand—who worship differently—who have a different skin color or sexual orientation. Nowhere, is the truth for who we can be more evident and encouraging than on the Camino de Santiago.

Soon I was walking with Martin, a grad student from Virginia, who had been slowed down with crippling pain in one of his knees.

"It's from an old injury I got while playing football in high school," he told me. "I had completely forgotten about it—assuming it had healed since there have been no symptoms in the past few years."

He admitted that he had been pushing to finish the camino as time and money were a factor. I did not need to remind him that walking twenty to thirty miles per day would cripple anyone—let alone someone with an old injury.

A mother and daughter from the UK joined Martin and me as we celebrated our walk with laughter and individual stories of pilgrimage. We talked of why we came and what we had learned. I gave Martin a day's supply of painkiller, taken from my earlier prescription, to ease his pain until the next pharmacy. Kristen and Kristi had walked with Martin the previous day and were joyous in finding him again, thankful that he had conceded not to walk thirty miles that day. I marveled at the friendship and thoughtful determination the two women shared—at complete ease and acceptance with each other. I suspected that they had brought the ingredients for such a strong relationship with them. The camino can only strengthen what we bring to it.

Tio Pepe is a private family run albergue located in the center of Villar De Mazarife, next to the church. It is small with only twenty-six beds housed in six rooms on the second floor. Downstairs is the bar and dining room where the home cooked meals and hospitality created one of the warmest home-away-from-home receptions on the whole camino.

To the side and rear of the bar, a walled and partially covered patio provided both sun and shade where we could relax, do laundry and socialize. Soon our little family was joined with Rose, a thirty year old from Ireland. She had left a marriage that didn't work to search for the girl she hoped was hiding inside. She had just begun to find her.

Soon, the tall double wood gates of the patio opened to admit another pilgrim—this one on horseback. The beautiful rider, a lady from Barcelona, dismounted, removed the saddle and began serving her handsome mount a bag of oats and water. In addition to walking and bicycling, horseback is the only other accepted form of travel on the camino. I had seen other equestrian pilgrims but this was the first time I had been housed with one. The wonderful animal was overwhelmed with love and attention from all of us.

That night, Spain would play Italy to retain its championship in the Euro World Cup Soccer games. The bar was filled with pilgrims and village locals, united in spirit and an allegiance that shouted itself hoarse until their team held the prize once again.

Our happy and quirky little family of five pilgrims set out together the next morning—walking on a timeless path with no one thinking of the destination. We were glad to share the journey—a bond and camaraderie of self-discovery as it was happening, at that moment, on a road every bit as magical as the one to Oz.

Late that day we came to a bridge that was a marvel to see, with a history that has inspired songs, poems and perhaps—even Cervantes to write his greatest epic. The thirteenth century Puente de Orbigo is the longest and best preserved medieval bridge in Spain. Its dozens of stone arches span the River Orbigo and its surrounding flood plain to the village of Hospital de Orbigo. The handsome horse that shared our lodging the night before was tethered on the far end of the bridge while his mistress had coffee on the terrace overlook.

The bridge is known as the Paso Honroso, or the bridge of honor, where one of the greatest medieval tournaments occurred in 1434. The Leonese Knight Suero de Quiñones scorned by his lady, wore an iron collar locked around his neck as a symbol of his love and bondage to her. To win her affection he challenged knights from all kingdoms to a joust on the Orbigo Bridge. He went to King Juan II and secured permission for the tournament where-upon the king's heralds rode out to proclaim the challenge and its conditions. The jousting began two weeks before St. James's Day which assured a large audience of pilgrims. We can only imagine the great spectacle that rose up around the bridge: a village of knight's tents, their colorful crests and pennants fluttering in the breeze. Squires would be bathing and exercising the many battle horses along the river, while knights clashed in practice battle in the meadows.

The tournament raged for over a month with jousts all day, feasts and dancing all evening. A week into the tournament, a Catalan knight appeared in double armor—boastful and with much swagger, he challenged Suero. Amused by the heavily armored knight, Suero mocked him by appearing in a woman's blouse over his own light armor. The enraged challenger managed to knock Suero off his horse with a lucky blow to the head. It appeared that all was over for our hero but to the cheers of the large crowd, he quickly recovered to win the joust.

Many knights on the way to Santiago stopped to challenge Suero but he remained victorious throughout the tournament. In the end, during a great celebration and processional, Suero proclaimed himself free of his bonds to the secret lady. He had broken the lances of three hundred challengers while wearing the iron collar of fealty and commitment. He and his knights rode to Santiago as pilgrims where he gave thanks

Talking With Cats

and presented the cathedral with a jewel encrusted gold bracelet. The bracelet is still there, around the neck of one of the saints in the cathedral museum.

The Romans bred and raised many thousands of cattle in Spain, and Orbigo was central to their passage through the region. Known as the Camino de la Canada, this was the equivalent of America's nineteenth century cattle drives from Mexico and the Great Plains through Kansas City. The Bridge of Honor has stood witness to the battle between the Swabians and the Visigoths in 452 and held strong when Alfonso III defeated the Moors on its banks in 878. The town belonged to the Knights Templar in the twelfth century and was later deeded to the Knights of Saint John of Jerusalem, who left their legacy of hospice and pilgrim care.

I parted company with my little family after they shopped for dried meats, fruits and cheese to fortify many more hours on the camino that day. "We're headed for Astorga," Kirsten told me as they sat on park benches bandaging blisters.

I was happy to stay at the Albergue Karl Leisner, a rambling historic building built around a flower bedecked courtyard. It had been renovated and was operated by a German Confraternity. After a grilled trout lunch, I gathered several sprigs of rosemary from the herb garden to stuff into my hiking boots. Refreshed with happy feet in cool sandals, I went in search of Órbigo's history and mystery.

The camino leaves Hospital de Órbigo onto a serene and naturally beautiful path through a valley and up into scrubland before arriving eight miles later at Astorga. Here, I walked into the capital of Maragato culture, where architecture, ruins and mysteries welcomed me with a little magic and a lot of awe and wonder.

In Astorga I found another Antonio Gaudi masterpiece. Yes, I have visited every one of his many jewels in Barcelona including La Sagrada Familia (Sacred Family Cathedral), several times. Leon lays claim to the palatial Casa Botines as an equal player in the pantheon of Gaudi architecture. However, for me, The Bishops Palace in Astorga is one of his greatest achievements.

It is a wonder of Neo-Gothic architecture with restrained splashes of Art Nouveau and Mudejar. The styles come together as an illusion—out of a dreamscape of what we might imagine such a building to be. It is a visual treat, inside and out, of balance, texture, and fantasy that satisfies from every angle, from every room and from every window.

The palace took so long to complete (1889-1913) that the Bishop died in the interim and the church never occupied it. During the Civil War it served as the regional Falange headquarters. Today I saw it as The Museum of the Pilgrimage of Santiago, which has been housed here since 1963. Nothing could be more appropriate. The palace walls hold an exceptional collection of two thousand years of history from the camino. The building alone is worth a visit to Astorga and coupled with the museum it is a knock-out.

The exterior is in small-block, rough-chiseled white granite with slim vertical stained glass windows. The whole achieves a sense of great height and fantasy while Gothic towers and turrets direct the viewer's gaze back to its grand Art Nouveau entrance.

Glazed brick trim, decorative tile and stained glass create vignettes of jewel-like proportions within tall airy rooms, some with Mudejar arches not unlike those in the famed Mesquita in Cordoba. In the private chapel of the Bishop's Palace, Gaudi has brought Neo-Gothic into a simpler state while still embracing the high naves and arches of Spain's great cathedrals.

Fortunately, a wise choice of art pieces and judicious placement allows both the art of architecture and the art on display to be best appreciated without confrontation. Gaudi finished the basement with the same elegant restraint of materials as the grander upper rooms. Here the museum has displayed Roman funeral objects including many sarcophagi, sculptures and mosaic flooring from ruins, found along the camino.

With the assistance of a policeman, I found my way to the Albergue St. Javier, a converted bit of antiquity in the old quarter near the cathedral. Astorga was like a toy store, and I just had to stay another day and play. I spoke with the hospitalera and asked for permission to stay an extra night. With my wish granted, I set about assembling the information and hours for a tour of the landmarks and restaurants that would become an adventure in Astorga.

Talking With Cats

Astorga is a town impossible not to like. Here is a lively market town of about twelve thousand who still celebrate their nomadic herdsmen with an annual sheep drive through the village streets. Remnants of the Maragato culture are strong. In the dark ages, these people were a vibrant culture with their own king. Their origin is uncertain with historians in disagreement—offering several possibilities. Some suggest that they descended from Goths who married into the Moorish culture; others say that they are from North African Berber tribes that remained behind in the mountains when the Moors were expelled. Today, they number but a few thousand spread among some forty remote mountain villages in the area.

One way to get to know a new culture is to eat their food and listen to their music. Astorga has a few restaurants that still prepare and serve the traditional Maragatan Feast. It would have been best to share my table with a friend or two but few pilgrims take time for a feast. No one could accept my invitation. It would take too much time, they told me.

The first part of the dinner was a large casserole of stewed meats—ten meats that is. There was beef, pork, chicken, duck, lamb, sausage and four organ meats that made up the ten. They had been braised and reduced through slow cooking to a fall-apart tenderness. The casserole was left on the table where I could take as much as I wanted. The next course was an even larger casserole of steamed vegetables which had been cooked with meat broth. The mixture was the traditional Maragato combination of cabbage, potatoes, onions and garbanzo beans. Dessert was a local feta type cheese and a sweet made from milk curds called *quamada*. The feast was served with a ceramic flagon of red wine and dessert was followed with boiled coffee laced with a mountain spirit similar to brandy. I had just suffered the misfortune of extreme gluttony.

Astorga has been at the junction of Spain's trade, commerce and pilgrimage routes for over two thousand years. The historic Silk Road and Spice Road trade came to the Iberian shores via its major port cities. The distribution spread across the land in exchange for its rich resources of olives, wine, grain, gold and herd animals. Caravans of goods from North Africa trafficked through the port at Cadiz, from the British Isles at Finisterre, through Portugal at Lisbon and Porto, from the Basque north coast at Santander and Bilbao, from Europe via the Pyrenees pass and the Mediterranean ports of Valencia and Barcelona.

When Santiago became a major pilgrimage site in the tenth century, Christians flowed on the well-established trade routes. All but those coming through Portugal converged at Astorga before entering the Galician mountains west to Santiago. The same is true today. The Primitive Camino through Asturias, the Via de la Plata from Seville and the Via Aquitania from central Spain come together here to join the Camino Francés for the final one hundred sixty-four miles to Santiago. There are at least twenty more feeder routes that converge from all directions into the three or four principal caminos.

During the height of its renaissance, Astorga had twenty-one hospices to service the thousands of pilgrims flowing through. It became a stop to rest, fortify provisions and prepare for the weather and the climb through the mountains of Galicia. It is believed that both Saint James and Saint Paul preached in Astorga. The hospice of San Roque hosted Frances of Assisi when he came through on his pilgrimage in 1214.

My second day here was richly rewarded with a tour of Astorga's historic Roman ruins, ten large plazas, architecture (especially the Baroque city hall), cathedral, churches and museums. Next to the Plaza San Francisco at the eastern entrance the delightful Jardin de la Sinagoga (Garden of the Synagogue) provided an enchanted bower of roses to rest beneath. The cathedral and its fine museum sit on the plaza opposite the Bishops Palace. They are well worth a visit for the architecture alone, as well as the large collection of art, jewelry and artifacts dating to the ninth century.

I went to bed early with thoughts of pilgrimage and what it means to not be traveling through a linear landscape—my path now led me from one adventure to the next with no consideration for time other than the rewards of food and sleep. How different it was when I had traveled in the past as a tourist: I entered each trip with a limitation which guided every day with how much I could see and do before departing for the rigid schedules required back at work and home. I never removed the clock-driven world of stress when I traveled.

14

LAND OF THE MARAGATO

*I would maintain that thanks are the highest form of thought,
and that gratitude is happiness doubled by wonder.*
~G.K. Chesterton

For the past few days I noticed that I had developed a new habit. I was so grateful to walk without pain or suffering that I started telling the various parts of my anatomy 'thank you.' Sometimes I even startled myself by saying out loud, "thank you hip, you're doing great today." For some magical reason, the more directly I focused my gratitude, the more rewards of joy in return—leading to more thanks—forming a circle of gratitude energy.

While walking one very hot day I became aware that my feet were hot and sweaty. They were not hurting, no discomfort, just an awareness of the steamy condition in my boots. I stopped at the next shady spot, removed shoes and socks and felt renewed with the cool breeze on my feet. I started to massage them and said out loud to each foot, "Thank you for giving me this adventure; I am very happy that we could do it together."

The pilgrimage had started to teach me that it was not "I" walking down that path—It was "We". We: the many parts that work together in the human body, to appear and function as one. Every day I found more to be thankful for. I learned that speaking gratitude was not necessary. If my thoughts truly visualized and felt the thanks, there would be an immediate feedback in the form of joy and pleasure. The Maragato Feast in Astorga tasted good—I felt thankful to be able to enjoy such an event. My body responded immediately as I savored the pleasure from every bite and sip. I sensed the nutrients and strength that were being "shipped out" to the many hungry parts of the whole. We were sharing the feast.

Giving thanks before a meal and meditating on thanks are positive rituals enjoyed in most societies and religions throughout the world and they have been part of my lifestyle since a child.

Here on the camino, I was learning how to use gratitude in a proactive personal relationship not only with my own body but with all things, all beings.

The wonderful Bishops Palace by Gaudi was such a pleasure to see that I felt grateful for the opportunity to be there. As in all creative works, I was able to visit an artist's dream realized. I didn't have to read about it or know the artist's thoughts—it was all there in front of me—in three dimensions—telling me its story. Every nuance of Gaudi's vision was manifest before me.

I did not send out a blanket gratitude for everything as we are taught to do in prayer. Gratitude became a personal connection that provided a two-way dialogue between me and what I was appreciating and accepting. When I stopped to admire a handsome rock, the immediate feedback was to sense and know the long journey that brought that rock to my hands. We knew each other. All I had to do was focus, accept, and be thankful, and the joy of knowing an object or being was immediate.

"Let us rise up and be thankful, for if we didn't learn a lot today, at least we learned a little, and if we didn't learn a little, at least we didn't get sick, and if we got sick, at least we didn't die; so let us all be thankful." ~Buddha

I did not arrive on the camino at age seventy-two without knowledge of history, cultures, world religions, literature, arts and how to function in the modern world. What became apparent was how little of my knowledge had been activated into wisdom. I have read that it is very important for babies to crawl—for in so doing they develop motor co-ordination and healthy right-brain, left-brain relationships. I think that walking also awakens the brain into its wisdom center where synergistic corollaries with body, spirit and the universe become available. It is evident that the level of acceptance, willingness to change and awakening to a universal wisdom is an individual choice; it can vary from a momentary flash—to sainthood or the kundalini of a Buddha. The operative, of course, must be to go beyond one's limiting concepts developed from the dogma of having lived the rigid rules of linear time.

During most of human evolution it has been necessary to observe the tribal rules of absolutes or perish. Along the way loyalty to the reigning gods and leadership were literally written in stone. Fear and mental watchdogs were established to make daily life easier. We knew the rules and didn't have to think—everyone in the tribe was united with the same software. There were no paradigm shifts; it took many generations to incorporate a new concept, a new god or goddess, or even a new food item. Differences were feared and demonized in others, usually leading to annihilation of the weaker group. Have we changed from that same model?

I have heard the computer hardware/software metaphor applied to people with the suggestion that it is our software that is limited. I don't think so; it is our hardware that limits us. Imagine trying to integrate modern digital software with its advanced graphics and global net into an early hardware system of 1990.

Many still hold the erroneous concept that our senses perceive all there is in the universe of sight, sound, smell, taste and touch. Actually, we have come to understand that our senses are but filters, allowing only the necessary wavelengths for limited function in an established physical linear existence. Today's science and technology have gone far beyond those limitations with travel among the stars, defining multiple universes, and quantum physics giving evidence that we create our own space/time continuum. We are still hardwired to fear changes (even the ones that can free us) and there is a strong fundamentalist movement across the planet to demonize and resist them.

Humans have evolved fearing the darkness and the unknown. Now we must face the most difficult transition and the widest, deepest chasm man has ever had to hurdle. We cannot do it as we were; it is beyond all the self-imposed limits that have governed our long progress. We can only enter the new paradigm as who we will become.

Walking the Camino de Santiago has taught me that for many; stepping into a brave new world will be welcomed as an adventure to discover the truth of our greater creative self. When we do, we become empowered by dimensions of being and thought that we have always known were there. We just couldn't find the doorway. For those ready to accept the light of change, the call to become compassionate gentle guides has never been greater. Marianne Williamson in her *Course of Miracles* said, "Our deepest fear is not that we are inadequate. Our deepest fear is that we are powerful beyond measure. It is our light, not our darkness, that most frightens us."

I left Astorga on July fifth with a clear blue sky and a temperature of just forty-six degrees. True to my guidebook's promise, the camino did have more traffic. Fortunately, some were strolling along at my pace and with an equal sense of adventure. One of my walking companions was a psychiatrist from Oslo, Norway. Matthew was well traveled, spoke several languages and amused us with many humorous and astute observations about life on the camino. An easy steady climb and the cooler temperature began preparing us for the mountains, soon to come.

At the hillside Maragato village of Murias de Rechivaldo we joined a crowd of pilgrims gathered at a bakery called El Llor. The baker, an Italian, came to Spain in search of a small village where she could raise chickens and bake. Here her dreams were manifest so perfectly that we pilgrims could only gasp in awe to find such a place on a remote dusty roadside. The counter was spread with beautiful pastries and mini sandwiches while the espresso's hot steam sang of cappuccino and frothy lattés. She greeted everyone in Italian with a welcome that made this little shop a piece of Tuscany. We grazed on pastries and heard many wonderful stories about raising chickens in a Spanish village. I was tempted to accept her invitation to visit for a few days of baking and chicken lore.

After another six miles, I stopped at the Maragato village of Santa Catalina de Somoza to spend the night at Albergue Hospederia San Blas. The suffix of Somoza is attached to many villages in the area—It means "under the mountain."

The next day I enjoyed a chilly walk to Rabanal Del Camino, a stone village clinging to the base of Mount Irago. It has a long history of caring for pilgrims before the steep climb up and over the weather ravaged mountain. I arrived at the Albergue Nuestra Senora Del Pilar in forty-five degree weather with high winds on July six. I could only imagine what it might be like on top. The kindly gentleman who greeted me said, "You should have been here yesterday when it was freezing." The desolate stone village combined with the weather could have been a stand-in for one in the foothills of the Himalayas.

I toured the town hoping for a tienda that might sell some warmer clothing items but there was nothing available, just one small grocer selling emergency provisions. Fortunately several hostels and restaurants offered excellent food service in restored buildings and monasteries. I made arrangements to have courier service transport my backpack over the mountain for five Euros each day and headed for lunch. La Posada Gaspar served a steaming sopa de fideos followed with a fine ragout of veal and flan for dessert.

I attended vespers at the Benedictine Monastery located in the twelfth century Santa Maria de la Asuncion—its six foot thick walls a sheltering welcome. It was a form of healing time-travel as the Gregorian chants filled the assembly with a meditation of medieval wonder. The monks have left the ancient stone walls, cracked and crumbling, with no adornments anywhere. There was nothing in the room save the rustic benches, a small crucifix, candles for light and a few red roses laid on the simple altar table. There was no electricity or other distraction of modern manufacture. None of the great churches and cathedrals that I had visited could equal the spiritual resonance of that sacred place.

There was an old stone building on a steep side street near my albergue that held a curious fascination for me. The sign simply stated,

"Italian Pub." A large dog lay across the entry offering a low growl to all comers. He did let me get close enough to see that they didn't open until six p.m. That night after vespers I broke my rule of no dinner at night and headed for the pub. The dog evidently knew the hours and moved to the side as I approached the door. Inside, one long, hand-hewn table filled the small room and a framed poster of Maria Callas was centered on the wall. A bar on the left held a full, dry aged Serrano ham, complete with the pig's foot attached, resting in its carving spit. A large round of local goat cheese sat on a board nearby. The back bar held a display of wines, baguettes of fresh bread and aperitifs.

I was greeted by a small compact gentleman in Spanish—his baritone accented with an unusual non-Italian inflection. A selection from La Traviata filled the small room as I was introduced and invited to be seated with the other guests, all from France.

The host carved thin shards of the aged ham and along with the cheese and bread served me an excellent red from Bierzo. A small card displayed my choices for dinner: four pasta dishes and that was all, there was no salad, no soup and no dessert. The price was the same for each of the pastas: five Euros. I ordered Pasta Carbonara. After the host left for the kitchen my tablemate said, "It will be quick—but they taste very good. He must have some way of reconstituting pre-cooked items."

The pasta was quick and delicious, and served with an aged parmesan, grated table-side. How can he do this for only five Euros? I thought. The opera selection changed to the Nessum Dorma aria from Puccini's Tournadot and I nodded my approval to the observant Giovanni, who was standing nearby. He spent the next hour putting on all his favorites to test my knowledge and see how fast I could name the opera and then the aria. He was puzzled: how was it possible for me to call his choices so quickly. "Surely, you are a musician or a singer?" he queried. I never did reveal my secret: I owned every album he was selecting, having played them over and over for more than twenty years.

Giovanni loved all things Italian including his choice of name. To serve Italian food he operated his pub with frozen entrees that were prepared al dente for him by a big city chef. His distinctive accent came from the Maragato language. I had made one of the most delightful new friends and enjoyed a superb dinner—with opera, for five Euros.

15

WILD DOGS OF FONCEBADÓN

*. . . The dog hurled himself at me and again pushed
me to the ground. This time he evaded the rock easily,
biting my hand and causing me to let it go.*
~Paulo Coelho, *the Pilgrimage*

Paulo Coelho's account of his journey on the camino came out in English in 1992 and Shirley MacLaine's bestseller *The Camino, A Journey of the Spirit* was published in 2000. Both authors give stirring accounts of their encounter with wild dogs while passing through the village of Foncebadón. Needless to say, many pilgrims who weren't armed with recent knowledge of the mountain town were fearful and planned their passage through in full daylight. Many suggested to new friends in Rabanal Del Camino that they travel in groups "just in case there were wild dogs hiding in the ruins." I planned to go no further; if there was a bed in Foncebadón I wanted to know more about this mysterious mist-shrouded Maragato village.

Mount Irago stands at just five thousand feet but often it acts like a malicious, much larger mountain. Even in summer, ice storms, strong winds and fog can be so thick that pilgrims lose their way. It is a steep mountain, possessing a strange and ethereal beauty, which feels more sacred than scary. I climbed to Foncebadón in full sunshine. At least seventy-five percent of the slate village is in some state of collapse. The remainder is in a frenzied state of repair and rebuilding—the village is on the comeback with four hostels and at least that many restaurants. I checked into a renovated monastery operated by the Monks of Domus Dei and headed out for exploration.

I confess that I had actually hoped for the swirling mists of a creepy village with the possibility of fairy tale witches huts—smoke curling out of their chimneys, while incantations from within call strangers to their spells. No such luck. This was one of the most pleasant and beautiful places on the entire camino. The old stone walls had crumbled to knee height, where I stood and watched a herd of eighty dairy cows graze on the plateau grasses dotted with colorful wild flowers. A mare and her colt rested within a few feet and the bray of a jackass nearby broke the stillness. One of the larger albergues had a shop with lots of food provisions, fresh fruit, local cheeses and bread from the city. A once abandoned city was very much alive. I saw only one small dog and he was wild alright, wild to have pilgrims rub his tummy.

There was one intriguing building in the village center that looked like it might have been a set piece from the movie *Lord of the Rings*. The signage appeared to have been installed during the reign of some medieval king and here there were curls of smoke coming out of the chimney. I opened the great heavy wooden door and entered La Taberna Gaia where I was greeted by a tall bearded gentleman who appeared to be half wizard and half woodsman.

"Bienvenido Don Caballero," intoned a sonorous basso profundo voice that seemed to come from the mountain itself "Aqui estamos La Cocina Medieval."

The décor, the menu, the service pieces were all handmade copies of a medieval hospice dining room and kitchen. The Medieval Kitchen was the brainchild of its owner and host, Don Enrique Notario. I was in shock. Not only had I never seen such a perfect reproduction of a historic era but set in the midst of such a remote village, it was truly inspired.

"How can you survive in such a remote location?" I asked Don Enrique.

"My dear sir," he replied, "they drive for fifty miles to dine here every day that the roads are open."

I feasted on a fine crock of winter squash soup and tender oven braised venison served over a bed of steamed potatoes with a garnish of grilled apples. A tankard of local crafted ale completed an unexpected gastronomic journey back to the twelfth century village of old Foncebadón. By midafternoon Don Enrique had a full-house of gourmands eager to feast on The Medieval Kitchen's fine mountain game and trout.

The Cruz de Fierro (Iron Cross) has been located at the peak of Monte Irago for many centuries. I decided to make the one-and-a-half mile hike that afternoon for a visit and meditation. The weather tomorrow morning might obscure everything and make a visit impossible. The original iron cross of medieval times is in the museum at the Bishop's Palace in Astorga. The cross today, like its predecessor, is of simple iron and standing atop a very tall weathered pole, where it has long consoled and guided pilgrims on their journey. It is surrounded with a twenty foot high pyramid of stones that are some fifty feet in diameter.

Early Christian pilgrims started leaving small prayer rocks and mementoes of family members, both those living back home and deceased. This tradition predates Christianity where pre-Roman Celts left piles of stones on mountains and sacred spots. The Romans had a similar custom leaving stone cairns in honor of the god Mercury. Today almost every pilgrim of every faith stops to meditate or say a prayer and leave some sacred object in memory of someone. I had carried shells, small stones and jewelry items from family and friends to leave as their presence and memory at the cairn of the Iron Cross.

I had arrived late in the afternoon, having met nor seen anyone else; I stood alone on the cold, windy peak humbled by the murmurs of long-a-go prayers. At sunset, the dappled cloud cover became a rose peach while I meditated and left the objects that I had carried for forty days on the camino. On the way back down the mountain I passed the ruins of a great pilgrims' hospice established by King Alfonso VI in the twelfth century. Cattle grazed in its courtyard.

Domus Dei had eighteen beds but that night only fourteen pilgrims were registered. Two wool blankets were on each bed and a small wood burning stove had been kindled to warm the small room. I was the only American with two young men from Slovakia, three Germans and the rest Spanish. The hospitalero kept the stove going while he prepared a spaghetti supper for everyone. The warmest of all was the kindness, acceptance and friendship of our little family. No one had greater wealth than we few pilgrims, gathered around a fire on a cold starry night on Mount Irago.

Everyone at Domus Dei was up by six; some had left even earlier and added new wood to our fire. I took my thermometer outside to read the temperature where the darkness and thick fog hid everything within three feet. It was forty degrees with strong winds on the eighth of July, my daughter's birthday and I was on a mountain with no internet or phone service to call her. I wanted to tell her where to search for my frozen body in case the storm gods finished me off.

No one was prepared for the weather that waited outside. Some of the girls were turning socks into mittens and garbage bags into rain gear. I put on three layers of shirts, a lightweight sweater, and a windbreaker jacket and tied a scarf around my head. I then put on my gloves and hooded rain poncho and tied the drawstring tight around my face before I stepped outside into the clouds.

I was grateful for yesterday's visit to the Iron Cross as the camino and intersecting farm roads and animal paths created a confusing maze in the fog. I could hear the bells on cows grazing nearby, confirming my location was near the ruins. There were small details and clues remembered from my earlier trip that guided my turns and steps as I climbed the mountain and passed where I knew the Iron Cross to be. Not even the cairn revealed itself until I stumbled into it. A pilgrim on horseback appeared like a ghost out of the mist beside me and vanished just as quickly, the horse carefully picking his steps around the many small stones.

The camino followed the ridge with little descent for three miles. The fog lifted to reveal another nearly abandoned village called

Manjarin. They have an albergue that can sleep thirty-five, a haven for those caught in mountain storms and fog. The gift that day was the views of pristine nature filled with abundant animal life, bird songs and wild flowers. I stopped to rest near a den of fox frolicking on the hillside with their kits.

A deer wandered by, seeming to know that she was safe. I wished for a book of birds of northern Spain, to help me identify the various species with their beautiful colors and songs. Many wildflowers were in bloom and the dominant mountain heather was so thick that it created a violet haze on the horizon.

Deep and steep gorges separated Mount Irago from its many neighboring mountains, some of them still shrouded with their own clouds. Occasionally a distant stone village would come into view. Other than that, there were no interruptions by man. There were no power lines climbing through the passes, no modern signage and no outposts of convenience to litter the landscape. Spain needs to be commended for protecting the land, flora and fauna of their countryside. How they prevent the encroachment of commercialism I do not know. I do know that in most industrialized countries, it would take a strong proactive environmental watchdog to beat back the invaders.

Coming down Mount Irago on the western slope is no easy task. The path is eroded, steep and full of loose flat shale that makes every step an opportunity to take a ride down the mountain on your backside. Grateful for having two trekking poles with steel points, I picked my way carefully—knowing that more injuries occur going downhill than up. I became aware of an immense headache—growing stronger by the minute, my first in many years.

The rocky path down the mountain turned into the principal cobbled street running through the stone village of Acebo. I fell into the Albergue Meson El Acebo ready to find healing and rest from the throbbing headache. While I waited in the bar/reception area the attendant prepared a coffee for another patron. Coffee, oh my God—that's it. That was my first day on the Camino without coffee. How sad to be an addict, I thought, as I ordered a double espresso.

Acebo was not at the bottom of the mountain, perhaps the steepest portion was behind me but the descent would continue for five more miles on rocky path. This time I was able to get coffee and breakfast before starting another day's adventure. I breezed through Riego de Ambros and rested at Molinaseca, a charming village hugging the western base of Mount Irago. From here to the Galician mountains I would be trekking through the great gardens, castles and vineyards of the Bierzo. The last big city before Santiago was just a few miles ahead.

Ponferrada is a city with a population exceeding sixty thousand. It straddles the convergence of the Sil and Boeza rivers with an immense castle crowning the ridge in the center of the old walled city. The camino path had to cross a wide expanse of RENFE train tracks as we entered from the east. Ponferrada created a novel approach to get the daily stream of pilgrims across the many tracks and switching lines. In other cities the solution had always been a pedestrian bridge. Here a green caged metal ramp climbed five levels before efficiently and safely funneling us across the hazards below.

The Albergue San Nicolas de Flue is operated by the Swiss order of the same name. The large modern hostel sits on the grounds of the Convento Del Carmen and can house two hundred ten pilgrims with four beds per room. The services included a fully equipped kitchen where we were invited to cook and share any food from their reserves. An extensive arbor-covered patio connected the convent, laundry facilities and hostel. After lunch, I headed for the castle.

The Knights Templar built the castle in Ponferrada on the ruins and same location occupied by a Roman fort and later a Visigoth fort. In 1218 the Templars, wealthy and strong, with a combined body of twenty thousand knights, started construction of the largest and best fortified castle in Spain. What was completed in 1282, stands today as proof and testament to what our fairy tales and movies have imagined castles to be. First, it is big, so big that it takes a mile long walk to circle the ridge that the castle completely covers—it is not possible to see the entire structure from the ground. Just the 172,200 square-foot castle proper is 314 feet wide and 538 feet long. On the west and north sides it rises up from the Sil River on sheer vertical cliffs and the other walls are fronted with a moat that is crossed by a drawbridge to the crenellated towers at the grand double entrance.

This castle served all the functions of a small village within its walls. It was a fort, a palace for the knights, an inn for travelers and pilgrims, a hospital for the sick, a restaurant and ale house for finding sustenance, and a monastery and chapel for worship. The central plaza housed trades such as blacksmiths and leather workers. There was a cemetery for proper burial and a dungeon for enemies and criminals.

The modern city of Ponferrada holds an annual celebration, when costumed actors return the castle to a day in thirteenth century medieval life and knights' banquet in the great hall. I wondered if late at night, ghosts patrolled the ramparts—longing for the days of chivalry.

That evening, San Nicolas became a sanctuary where pilgrims of many nationalities drifted from table to table, from group to group, from patio to the garden and back. It was a feeding frenzy of seekers and likeminded pilgrims joining discussions on spirituality, ecology, and philosophy. We were like a collection of hummingbirds looking for the finest nectar as it flowered from the assembled minds and hearts. Some of the hostel staff on the entrance patio sang and played guitar to a rapt audience of joyful celebrants; their blisters and trail injuries forgotten in the moment. I joined a group discussion under the arbor.

We all agreed that at this point in walking the camino, we were changing. Some felt the need to talk with their families; others had been able to find solutions to complicated relationships.

"I don't understand why I didn't think of it before," a young man from Switzerland said, "Yesterday, on the mountain, it just came to me—such a clear thought—I came to the camino unsure of what I wanted to do in life. Today, I have a dream. I'm excited to go back and get started."

An engineer from India jumped in "I feel like the one hundredth monkey and I just washed my first sweet potato."

"Yes, we're all washing our first sweet potato and making a good meal out of it, at that," said another, with a hearty laugh for all.

During the first few weeks, many pilgrims spent the evenings treating blisters and complaining of pains and other hardships of the moment. That was no longer true. We were pulling together; every night it was a different group at a different hostel but instantly we became like family. Not only were we finding common ground, each of us was experiencing a personal awakening and was excited to share the newly defined self. Soon we were in a spirited debate on the teachings of Chardin, and the new paradigm of becoming global and cosmic.

In 1973, I was in the hospital for a few weeks with an illness that was not life-threatening but required rest. One day Dr. John Sloan walked in and presented me with a book, *The Phenomenon of Man* by Pierre Teilhard De Chardin. He said "I think you are ready for what this Jesuit priest and scientist has to say. Let me know what you think." There was no time for discussion. He gave me a knowing smile, turned and continued his rounds. We never got to have that talk; soon I was back to work, moved to another city and Dr. Sloan passed away. How many teachers come into our lives every day without our ability to recognize them? Forty years later, I have read Chardin and I am ready for that discussion, Dr. Sloan.

Chardin introduced the term "noosphere" in 1922 to denote the sphere of human thought. For him, the noosphere emerges with the synergistic interaction of human thought. The noosphere evolves as mankind evolves and organizes itself into higher social networks and knowledge. Today, ninety years later, science and spirituality are converging to advance the concept of the inevitable emergence of global human consciousness. In many ways we are the seed for what we are to become. Chardin suggested that we are a whole new species, unique in the biosphere, evolving in ways we do not understand. We only see the shadow, not the creature. Will it be of transcendent light or darkness of matter?

The concept of global thought and co-operation is not an attractive possibility as long as so many societies are imprisoned with dogma and irrational rules based on primal prejudices. In the first quarter of the twenty-first century we either remain clusters of adolescents who refuse to put the old toys and war games away, or we grow up to take positions of responsibility. If each religion must retain its own god, will those gods eventually battle it out? Will the winner take all?

What we can do is be observant for groups and societies that are taking positive action to aid and assist their people. They want to become responsible players on the global stage. Action is something we can see; it has gone beyond the game of rhetoric. These new societies will be inclusive and open to diversity with an enthusiasm to heal and protect the species and environment of earth. We need to focus our attention, resources, and wisdom towards assisting and supporting those people, those groups, those nations. Our future, as well as theirs, depends on achieving a sustainable healthy planet through co-operation, acceptance and trust.

There is another silent enemy running among all of us that dims the vision for a brave new paradigm. That demon is called apathy. We beings of light are everywhere in all countries; we are the scientists, theologians, technologists, educators, politicians, artists, environmentalists, workers and citizens at large. We have been invaded and rendered helpless under a constant media blitz of wars, genocide, wanton slaughter, terrorism, oil spills, poisoned water supply, global warming and incurable diseases. The best any of us can do "is to stick our finger in the dyke." The collective is so great that our human filters close down, overwhelmed with the horrors of such magnitude, we are rendered helpless. Noam Chomsky has said, "All over the place, from the popular culture to the propaganda system, there is constant pressure to make people feel as though they are helpless, that the only role they can have is to ratify decisions and to consume."

Apathy has reduced us to frustrated individuals and small groups unable to overcome the oppression of materialism, governments, terrorism and greed. The reason: we do not have a framed vision to unite us. By remaining fractured, we have no voice. We all speak a different language—though we may well speak the same truth. When the dream and the vision for our future are framed in a universal language, the people will awaken and become a united force of change. Nothing short of a global revolution will take us there. The vision for that change is ready to lead us; it only requires unity in numbers. In the meantime, we remain huddled behind the great walls of an imagined prison constructed with bricks of fear, stones of prejudice and dogmatic belief systems. Are we waiting on another Messiah or are we ready to look in the mirror and accept the truth, "it is me, it is us, we are one."

It is also important to frame our offensive in an articulate and acceptable format that has a universal resonance of truth. The banner of the new paradigm must herald its wisdom and vision in symbols and metaphors that are inclusive, that will give everyone the courage to make the transition. We cannot move forward finding fault with what we know is wrong—there is too much, we become defeated with the sheer volume. Every day the press reports how the opposition has new reinforcements. By allowing ourselves to be drawn into the conflict we are forced to demonize "the other," to keep the old wounds raw and open. In the art of war, we strengthen the opponent by standing on the opposing shore calling him names.

The worst tragedy of all is that good people and resources are wasted. They are neutralized by entering the war of resistance in a defensive position. The mere act of participating depletes the spiritual energy of vision and wisdom, reducing it to a material level where the darkness will always be the winner. Light must support light. When the collective is greater than the darkness, we will break through to the new paradigm as authentic activated beings. Darkness cannot be fought with its own rhetoric of negative suggestion and Orwellian miss-speak. It does disappear under the light of truth, wisdom, vision and empowered leadership. When the breakthrough comes, many defenders of the old paradigm will make the conversion, claiming the new state of being as their own. For others, it may take generations.

"There are not only minds on the earth. The world continues and there will be a spirit of the earth . . . . Why do we hesitate to open our hearts wide to the call of the world within us, to the sense of the earth?" ~Pierre Teilhard De Chardin, *Human Energy*

16

WAYS OF THE WAY

*If I am dependent on the behavior of others for my
sense of serenity, I will never become free.*
~John Brierley, *A Pilgrim's Guide to the Camino de Santiago*

It is one thing to walk for four hours among the vineyards of the Bierzo but quite another to stand atop a hill and watch them cross valleys, climb hills and disappear on all horizons. The sheltered micro-climate of the region uniquely lies between the humidity and rains from coastal mountainous Galicia and the hot dry plains of Castile for an ideal vine culture. The Romans introduced vineyards into the region but it was the monasteries that widely distributed the culture to include Galicia and Asturias.

Spain has consumed the majority of the regions production until recently, when wider distribution in Europe and America created a new fan-base. Every restaurant and bar along the region's camino serves a refreshing new crop selection from one of several varieties. Reds from the Mencia grape and a light flowery white from the Doña Blanca are favorites. I attended a tasting of some oak barrel aged red, which deepened the character and earthiness without adding the "oaky" taste to the mix. They also harvest a Merlot and Cabernet Sauvignon that competes well on the global stage. I waved to farmers planting and tilling new vines on every plot of vacant Bierzo earth they could find.

I walked through the village of Cacabelos and across the bridge on the western side to stay at the Capilla de Las Angustia, a very unique and welcoming home for the night. The eighteenth century church had a fortified gated wall completely surrounding the complex and courtyard. A row of thirty-five chalets, each housing two persons, formed a semicircle inside the walled arena. Most pilgrims that night were from France, Germany and Spain with a few from Japan. The lone American, I shared a room with a Frenchman who could neither speak nor understand Spanish or English. I was surprised that he and his wife had made the journey without learning even the most common greetings in their host country's language.

Restaurant cuisine had started to become Galician, most choices being seafood with a strong emphasis on mussels and octopus. Pulpo (octopus) Gallega is more popular from the Bierzo through Galicia than hamburgers and French fries are in the states. In fact, it is standard to be served in two sizes, small appetizer and large as an entrée. The method of preparation and presentation is always the same: coin sized rounds of steamed tentacle are cut into one inch pieces, drizzled with olive oil, sprinkled with a grated red pepper, and served on a wood plate. I ordered a plate of mejillones (muscles) and a small plate of pulpo. The freshness of both and the tenderness of the octopus gave abundant testimony to the integrity of simple uncluttered preparation with truly fresh ingredients.

We were only one hundred twenty miles east of Santiago. At this juncture my fellow pilgrims seemed to divide into four categories. For many in the first category, like the group embroiled in healthy debate the night before, their pilgrimage had become a release from stress and rigid linear timelines. In their new relaxed state of acceptance, questions and concerns were becoming answers and solutions. They had surrendered to the pilgrimage and its teaching.

For others in the second category, fears and demons remained a daily challenge which often resulted in a complaint or angry judgment call on others. Rather than release fears and allow the demons of the past to escape, these few held on to their old baggage where they found fault with the food, weather, accommodations and each other. They greeted newcomers with a long litany of limitations and handicaps, held aloft like a shield—with acceptance and pride. Their message said, "We are walking the camino not to awaken and lighten our load, but to prove we can carry our many burdens. They are our reality and we become stronger for carrying them." In fact, those very words are a quote from one long-suffering soul.

The third group was those who came to walk or cycle the camino in the quickest and most efficient manner possible. They came for a healthy adventure in whatever their vacation time allowed. Among this group I met the vice president of a major European auto manufacturer, bankers, doctors, and young corporate executives. They could afford the best of trekking gear and often stayed in fine hotels for privacy and a hot tub bath. They listened to their bodies, repaired what hurt and enjoyed the journey for all the challenges and geographic splendor it held. They celebrated with each other over good food, wines and sports events in the camaraderie of fine restaurants and pubs. They were not on a life-changing pilgrimage, any dysfunction or fear had been left at home.

The fourth group was not present during the first half of my pilgrimage. They were mostly Spanish and European families, vacationing with their children and parents for the final stage of the camino. They had planned their trek to arrive in Santiago during the week of celebrations for Saint James day on July twenty-fifth.

One gentleman with just one leg walked with the aid of crutches and had his teenage son for a companion. A father, with family members, pushed his daughter's wheelchair the entire distance of one hundred thirty miles from Ponferrada. A gentleman of seventy-eight was unable to carry his backpack. Even though he was with his wife and several family members, he insisted on pushing a wheeled cart up and down the mountain paths. I spoke with him several times over a two week period. He told me, "It is easy; I only take one step at a time."

Also in the fourth group were collections of teenagers, some from churches, and others with just school friends. They jogged, sang, laughed and played their way to Santiago. Their wholesome energy added a contagious spirit of celebration and joy as they skipped through the forest. Tour buses were also plying the roadways that parallel the camino, stopping at all significant landmarks and historic towns. Their goal was also to arrive festival week. Their occupants, unable to stay at official hostels, were booked into local hotels.

Due to the many families, elderly and disabled that were walking from this stage forward we had a new service. Taxis would deliver, for a small fee, our backpacks to the next location. All hostels participated by providing special luggage tags and envelopes to hold the standard five Euro fee for each bag. The next day we left with just a daypack and our trekking poles. In the mountains of Galicia, I had been rescued.

I reflected on my own growing abilities to center, observe, accept and remain in the present without judgment. As I became more aware and began to accept these gifts of being in the moment, the more others sought me out to be with, to talk with and to share stories from their own journey. I was not the teacher; I was the student, in school working on my own masters in awareness, acceptance and being. In some ways, I actually felt selfish by creating an environment that would attract the teachers to me. Every pilgrim, every stone, path, animal, flower and ruins had a long story to tell; their journey was written in an open book. I was learning to read it.

Had I been able to order a day in paradise, the walk from Cacabelos to VillaFranca would have been a top contender. The profusion of vineyards, an endless patchwork of intersecting vertical and horizontal plantings, created a pleasing harmony and discipline for the eye to fall upon. The young green leaves and vines held infant bunches of pea-sized grapes that sprouted from ancient gnarled bases, the size of a man's leg. For me the Bierzo was a mythical garden, a place where I imagined that wars, chemicals and discord never entered. With the misty mountains of Galicia hovering on the horizon, I might have been in Shangri-La.

VillaFranca Del Bierzo has more history and stories than possible to cram in one book. Suffice it to say Castros (stone-age Celtic villages) have been found here, with the Romans, Moors, and Visigoths following in succession. Its location at the confluence of the Burbia and Valcarce rivers became strategic and vital with the Bierzo valley to its east and the mountain pass through O'Cebreiro to its west. It has been ruled by a long succession of nobles and had a monastery founded by Saint Francis of Assisi. A castle built in 1490 for the Marquesas' de VillaFranca still stands on the eastern side of the town.

Like many medieval towns with advantageous geographic locations VillaFranca has suffered numerous setbacks. In additions to the warring nations hungry for its power base, the town was decimated with the plague in1589, floods in 1715 and suffered unbelievable carnage by the English in 1809. They wrecked the castle, robbed the churches, and burned the municipal archives.

Despite everything I have told you, the hillside town has incredible charm, a welcoming Plaza Major with good restaurants, and a downtown park that is filled with well-tended aromatic gardens overflowing with flowers. Many of its churches and monasteries have unique architecture and art worthy a day's visit. The cobblestone streets wind and twist as they flow through the town, and always present exciting new views of architectural detail and village life.

I walked through the town, crossed over the Burbia River on an ornate iron bridge and took a private room at the charming Albergue de la Piedra. My sunny room overlooked the river and the rocky cliffs of the Galician piedmont. I stepped out to explore the city and ran into an old friend from a few days back.

I had met Hans coming down Mount Irago. He was a teacher from south of Oslo, Norway and was walking with his brother and sister-in-law. Hans and I stayed in the same hostel in Acebo while the couple luxuriated in a hotel with bathtub. We had the same hip problem which led to long discussions on American health care and Norwegian life. He had walked the camino before and was upbeat and excited to be back as a pilgrim. Despite having had two heart attacks and hip injury, Hans at age sixty-one was one of the most optimistic pilgrims on the whole pilgrimage. We agreed to meet later for lunch in the plaza.

Over lunch, I discovered how we were able to meet again. Hans' sister-in-law had fallen and injured her ankle requiring a few days rest. He would resume his trek alone the next day and rendezvous with them later where they would catch up by bus. On the way out, we were greeted by Fran and Annie, two American women from California that we both knew from Acebo. They were dining in the patio with a friend of theirs—Ramon, a tall, bearded professor-type from San Francisco. He was traveling in an extended family group of fourteen. Ramon, his wife, three children in high school and college were all walking with their best friends. None of them were intentionally walking together. They only agreed where to meet each night.

I love water—the ocean, dramatic thunder storms, rivers, lakes and long soaks in giant bathtubs. I do not enjoy getting wet in the rain. Wet clothes on my body have always been distasteful and I would rather be naked than keep them on. It is not a phobia, just an unhappiness and discomfort that I avoid. So far, forty-five days into the pilgrimage, I had not been rained on. Almost, but I had always made it to a village or into my hostel during the few downpours. I went looking for a larger poncho and a waterproof spray for my boots. I had been warned; Galicia is so wet that pilgrims have been known to melt and flow down the mountain.

The camino offered a choice of three paths for the next day's walk. The first followed the new super highway through the narrow Valcarce valley; the second choice followed the mountain ridge to the north of the valley; and the third choice was the most difficult trail winding up and around mountains on the south side of the valley. Both mountain paths came with warnings of their difficulty and remoteness from villages, food and assistance. The caveat to both was the rugged natural beauty of the piedmont. I decided to climb the mountain trail to the north which would descend into the valley village of Trabadelo.

My friends of the day before had gathered at the base of the cliff where I would begin my climb into the remote north mountains. They had chosen the safe, highway route as Hans spoke for all of them, "If I had an accident or heart attack up there, it would be over." They all bid me farewell with hugs and wishes for my safety as though I were going to trek through the desert for forty days. "We hope to see you soon," Annie called out from the roadway—hardly words of encouragement.

Perhaps fifty yards up the trail there was an official sign lettered on a weathered board. "Warning, be aware that this is a very steep and difficult climb. If you suffer from heart conditions, injury or are elderly, please take the valley road." At that point it was very steep with the narrow path mostly carved out of sheer rock. I had sent my backpack forward by taxi and felt confident and full of energy and enthusiasm for adventure. I was ready for this mountain, its poetry was calling me; besides, the highway path looked like an assignment for a prison work detail.

The path's steep beginning and the many warnings were symbolic of much of our lives. We err on the side of caution and follow the crowded roadway through the narrow rock faced valley until we die. Where did we get the group-think mentality that safer is the wise option? Do we no longer feel the stirring within for discovery, adventure and the courage to find excitement in the unknown? Homo sapiens may have evolved with primal programs of fight or flight intact but has he surrendered curiosity and the eternal search for magic and mystery on planet earth?

Soon the trail was above the rock cliffs and became less steep as it lead through lush, low vegetation, wildflowers and fields of butterflies. As I approached the ridge, the views into the valley and across to the alternate trail, working its way around cliffs and peaks, presented a powerful confirmation of my decision. Far below, pilgrims, appearing small as ants, were picking cautious footings on a hard path caught between the river and metal barriers of the highway. Sheer vertical cliffs rose on both sides of them.

Once the trail reached the ridge, the remainder of my walk became an enchanted journey where I encountered just three other pilgrims for its seven miles of panoramic views, forests and altars. At the summit of each peak many small altars or cairns of artfully stacked stones carried on the Celtic tradition of offerings to the gods and goddesses of nature. Some were very old and weathered but not all. Pilgrims have continued the tradition with small personal altars to family, the saints, Buddha and Jesus.

One altar had been built against the side of a gnarled pine tree with great care and Zen awareness. A small votive candle had been placed inside. I left a small personal token and lit the votive for a few minutes of meditation on gratitude. The word *gratitude* has always been common to my vocabulary and easy to use. Now, for me, gratitude and thank-you have become much more than words, they are much more than thoughts, more than prayers and greater than other forms of empowerment. Like mindfulness, gratitude is a state of being and through it we are humbled to become one with all beings. Gratitude can be the gateway to enlightenment.

My world had become filled with wonder and I with thanks for it. I think the awareness that we live in a universe larger than our mental grasp is liberating and allows wonder to become part of our daily journey. Wonder may be unique to Homo sapiens. It certainly is a gift that can save us from the labels, dogmatic beliefs, and fact-obsessed societies that control most cultures. One thing is for certain: if you don't believe in magic and wonder, you are correct: There is an abundance of facts to support your choice and you won't be lonely for neighbors. However, if you do remain open and receptive to wonder, your life may be filled with joy, happiness and infinite possibilities. We do have a choice and we are both right—only the outcome is different. Such is the power of thought.

The final third of the walk was through a type of woodland that I had never seen. A great forest of chestnut trees formed a canopy of shade and sanctuary, covering the mountains on the north side of the valley. (As a child growing up in Appalachia, my grandfather and his peers told many stories and legends about the mighty chestnut. They were all destroyed by a blight that swept America so fast no tree was left standing within a decade.) I reveled in their stately trunks, dark green foliage, patterns of bark and the abundant crop of nuts that was still on the ground. When ripe, the nuts fall out of their bristled outer shell when they hit the ground to form a crunchy double layer under all the trees. Several fires had been built along the path using the outer shells to roast the fat mahogany colored nuts.

I found a smooth rock under one of the chestnut trees, where I sat enjoying a few dried apricots, almonds and spring water. Two very large crow-sized birds flitted through the canopy giving only a partial glimpse of grey and brown feathers. I never did see an entire bird to know its name. I thought the mystery might be more important than learning my bird's identity. Maybe, it was my totem for that day, a trickster bird that would cleverly lead me to my next truth.

17

MOUNTAIN OF MIST

All journeys have secret destinations,
of which the traveler is unaware.
~Martin Buber

I left Trabadelo on Friday the thirteenth of July in sunshine and lots of bright blue sky. Ahead was the Galician mountain, which all pilgrims must cross to enter the misty lands of Celtic Spain. It took a defiant stance, crossed its arms, shaded its face in mist and waited. I was not intimidated, having already turned the threats of a difficult climb into one of my best on the camino. I imagined that perhaps this mountain also, just had a bad reputation, but was actually capable of being nice sometimes. I hoped that this would be one of his good days. After all, had I not been blessed with the guidance and protection of flow?

My path followed twelve miles of river and passed through seven villages before I began the ascent. Every hour the mountain assembled more clouds at its peak—obviously preparing for an afternoon assault. I stopped for some fortifying Bierzo wine and an assortment of local sausages at a patio in the last Castilian village of Herrerias. I watched in amazement as the mountain pulled the cloud mass down to its waist and waited again. This was not going to be one of his good days; he was getting dressed for war.

The mountain rose steeply with the only opportunity for relief at two small hamlets a short distance up the slope. The path was rutted, muddy, often narrow and very steep. For the first time since the Mountain of Forgiveness I had to work hard to stay off my ass. My breathing was labored and my heart was racing to handle the challenge. Thank God, my backpack had been shipped by taxi.

A young Spaniard from Seville was in front; having great difficulty pushing his bicycle up the slippery slope, where the muddy rut of a path was often bisected with great tree roots and rocks the size of sofas. His shorts and tee shirt were saturated in sweat, which revealed a very athletic frame of muscles—yet the job of getting up the mountain had reduced him to a bent-over panting weakling. As I came abreast equally exhausted, we could only stare at each other, breathing was more important.

Soon he said, "Sir, I don't know how old you are but you are certainly older than my twenty-two years and you are doing great."

Surprised, I could only say, "I am? Thanks."

The mist came down to us, swirling like giant, moist ghosts of serpents. As the rutted trail began to disappear, we came to the first outpost with lights on at the café and refuge. The mist had begun to leave droplets of water on my poncho as I joined two fellow pilgrims for wine and coffee. Karen was from California and Tom was from London. They had joined forces a few cities back and both felt more secure walking together. Tom said that he was actually glad to have the excuse to use his expensive new raingear for the first time. Karen had nothing except a small disposable plastic jacket that barely passed her waist. Worse still, she had no cover for the backpack that she was carrying. "I guess that I will have to take a few days to dry everything out," she told me.

We stepped outside the refuge into total whiteout. There was mist, fog, rain and clouds; all suspended together into absolute wetness. It hung suspended and motionless. It was both beautiful and terrifying as it obscured all traces of path, up, down or over the hillside. This was

Galicia's long heralded welcome. The temperature dropped with every step I took until my thermometer read forty-five degrees. Karen and Tom waved goodbye and disappeared into the mist, our paths never crossed again.

Small Celtic farms clung to the mountain cloaked in clouds, mist and rain. I knew the farms were there because I would bump into their barns on the roadside or encounter a ghost cow in my path. Worse still, was the slipping and falling in the wet cow droppings that peppered the path.

My hopes of remaining dry with three layers of clothes, a nylon windbreaker and heavy full-length poncho were pure fantasy. The air itself had become water; my poncho was dripping inside as much as outside. The trees dripped, the wind blew and the temperature dropped to forty degrees. The wetness turned into icy pellets of rain. Fortunately the barbed wire fence followed the steep path up the mountain and gave identity to what otherwise lurked in total obscurity. That day the claustrophobic thick cloud never lifted. I surrendered to the wetness as it soaked my clothing and ran into rivulets down my spine.

For some strange reason, I felt totally happy. I was chilled and soaked to the bone but thrilled and mystified by my surroundings, a Twilight Zone setting of a medieval Celtic movie. On top of the mountain, I entered the flagstone streets of O'Cebreiro, the lanterns and ancient stone buildings began to tell me even more about my new fantasy come-alive. The fog and rain added drama as the early twilight settled in on a village that was beyond my wildest imagination. I peeked into one stone building where a great hammered copper pot covered the entire surface of the glowing wood-fired stone cook-pit. "It's Pulpo Gallega (octopus, Galician style) for supper," called the cook.

In Galicia the pilgrim albergues are all run by the region and are called Xuntas (pronounced shun-tas) in the Gallegan language. They are either modern purpose-built structures or, in the smaller villages, converted school houses. I checked into the very modern steel, glass and stone two-story structure on the west side of the village. In Galicia, pilgrims can always count on consistent, clean, well-managed hostels with hot showers, internet and kitchen facilities. Never had I been more thankful for those services than in O'Cebreiro.

Soon, I was in dry clothes back at the big copper pot of pulpo. The cook brought me a stone bowl of cabbage and potato soup simmered in a rich broth. After a crusty chunk of the local rustic bread, a plate of pulpo dusted with red pepper and a cup of red wine, the chills had completely vanished. I was about to leave when the red-haired cook brought a large round of the famous O'Cebreiro cheese to my table. "Fresh, from the farm just down the road," she told me while serving up a large slice. "Why don't you try it the way we eat it, with wild mountain heather honey?" she encouraged.

The pleasure of a superb meal is rare anywhere but here in the swirling mists of Celtic country it was an experience of ecstatic proportions. I slowly ate and savored every morsel of the cheese and honey combination, both of exceptional quality and nuanced complexity. The cheese was creamy yet broke into crumbles and had a touch of sourness—that begged for more of the honey. Its dark aromatic character tasted of both flowers and herbs. "Sir, you cannot go out into the cold rain without a cup of our coffee with local brandy to ward off the chill," the cook said as she set a cup of the infusion at my table before returning to the glowing wood-fired open kitchen.

"When you are inspired by some great purpose, some extraordinary projects, all of your thoughts break their bonds. Your mind transcends limitations, your consciousness expands in every direction and you find yourself in a new great and wonderful world. Dormant forces, faculties and talents become alive, and you discover yourself to be a greater person by far than you ever dreamed yourself to be." ~Patanjali, *from the Yoga Sutras*

I awoke to discover a different O'Cebreiro: There was light fog, but more importantly, there was no rain or wet mist, small windows of blue sky held the promise of sunshine. Once again I sent my backpack forward via taxi and headed to the stone cottage for more local cheese with wild heather honey.

Yesterday, I was baptized in the traditional Galician triple waters of fog, mist and rain. It must have been a rite of passage and an awakening that I needed, because even though I had been soaked and chilled to a bone-shaking chatter, I was euphoric and happy. I went to sleep that way and I woke that way; this was a new enhanced state of being and

I liked it. I became aware of a subtle flow of energy moving from the earth, up through my body and out the top of my head as though I had become an electrical conduit. Maybe, this is what it really means to have taken the waters of O'Cebreiro.

I left the village through a forest where patches of mist still clung to the earthen path, bordered with ferns and wildflowers. I had lingered over cheese, bread and coffee that morning, talking with a new friend from Canada. Most of my fellow pilgrims had made their way out of town much earlier. I was thirsty to drink in this magical, otherworldly place alone and undisturbed. When I cleared the forest, the trail circled the ridge where a panoramic vista of valleys and neighboring mountains came into full view. The clouds formed a variety of patterns; some clung to the valleys, some formed crowns on mountain tops and others formed rings around their midriffs. I stood at the top of a very steep cliff where small animal paths went straight down the mountain connecting the hamlets and farm complexes that dotted the mountain side.

Six cyclists burst out of the forest and skidded to a halt just a few feet from where I stood on the steep overlook. They dismounted and formed a team huddle, obviously making plans for the day with maps and frequent checks on the view to the valley below. The actual Camino path followed the ridge before taking the plunge downhill via many switchbacks to reach the valley where it paralleled the highway to Triacastela—some thirteen miles to the west. The cyclists mounted their bikes and lined up on the path a hundred yards back in the woods and one by one launched themselves into the air high over the cliff's edge. Talk about overcoming one's fears and living in the moment. I watched in amazement as all six landed safely and hurtled by cows, goats and farmhouses to disappear into a blur—on a straight vertical descent to the valley far below.

It was mid-July yet the blackberries had just finished their bloom with the new fruit still tiny little beads of promise. I passed many gardens where no crop was ready to eat, not even the peas and tomatoes. Two days before, in the warmer Bierzo, I had walked through many cherry orchards where the abundance of ripe fruit covered the Camino in a bath of crushed crimson. In the village market they were for sale at one Euro per kilo.

Here on the mountain and in nearby villages, the animal culture was cattle. They graze on the rich mist-fed mountain meadows during the day—at night a family herdsman bring them home for milking. Often the home and barn form a single connected complex where the cattle are sequestered inside the barn portion. Morning and night the animals are moved out and back using the same Camino path as we pilgrims. We met a lot of cattle with their herdsman, and we dodged a lot of manure along the way. Sometimes dodging was not an option, standing up was.

That morning I had met a thirty year old Pakistani who lived in Canada. He was owner of a successful consulting firm and had taken a one year sabbatical to explore the world. We shared stories as he joined me for a cheese and honey breakfast slathered on hot crusty stone baked bread. Like many others his age who I had met walking the camino, his search was a quest for spiritual and personal truth.

They are wanderers in search of a meaningful life, smart people with considerable knowledge and education acquired from empirical facts, dogmatic religions and suppressive dysfunctional politics. They are no longer appeased with the global status-quo of materialism, doublespeak, war and poverty. Within them, a singular voice cries out for a personal story, a myth and a few mysteries that don't beg for a solution.

"Since starting my quest, I am learning to trust and open my awareness to being in each and every moment, said my friend. I don't have any plans other than to be open for guidance from the path itself. So far, in five months, it has taken me across three continents."

His comments reminded me of the story about an old wise man who said, "I learned everything there was to know in the world by the age of forty but alas, it took another forty years to unlearn it. Only then could I start at the beginning."

Later during my walk, I reflected on the morning conversation and Herman Hesse's *Siddhartha* which I was reading for the third time in fifty years. In one of his finest teachings to Govinda Siddhartha tells him; "Seeking means: to have a goal; but finding means: to be free, to be receptive, and to have no goal." My Canadian friend did not have goals; he like me was on an odyssey, a quest of discovering an authentic life along the way.

The camino remained on higher ground during the entire seven miles of that day's journey. It followed ridgelines, mountain streams and continued around the flank of another mountain into the hamlet of Fonfria where I spent the night. The settlement was nothing more than a collection of stone farmhouses and barns grouped around a central dirt road that also was the pilgrims' camino. On the way in I stood aside as two herders, one a teenager texting on his smartphone, took their cattle to the meadows.

Nailed onto a post near my xunta there was a hand lettered sign on a piece of tin, "Local Food, Last House." After a shower, I headed out to the last house. I had to carefully pick my way through the cow piles which covered the muddy village road. The aromas of warm milk—fresh from the cows, churned butter and the pungent sourness of fresh cheese filled the air as I passed several barns to get there.

A woman was preparing sandwiches and cheese for two pilgrims at the bar as I entered. They were going through without rest for another seven miles to Triacastela and planned to eat as they walked. I waved to the proprietor and took a table near the wood-burning stove. I took advantage of the time alone to imagine the old farmhouse's story and how it came to be the last house and only house serving local food to passers-by. Outside of building the small bar, little change would have been necessary to become a remote stop for hungry pilgrims.

Looking very professional in a blue dress and large white apron, the kind woman greeted me most warmly with a welcome to her house. "What have you prepared for a meal?" I inquired. "Not many pilgrims have time to sit for a meal," she told me "But I have made a Gallegan bean soup for the family that I think you will enjoy. After that I can prepare local chorizo, eggs and potatoes; and, of course we have fresh cheese and honey from the farmer next door. Will that be okay?" She brought a bottle of wine with the soup. I was humbled and honored to be on a magical journey that served me with such gracious hospitality. My heart could only feel gratitude.

18

AMBUSHED BY A HORSE

*Like all great travelers, I have seen more than I remember,
and remember more than I have seen.*
~Benjamin Disraeli

Triacastela has little to show for its namesake. The three castles of medieval times are in ruins, if you can find them at all. Nevertheless, the stone village has an abundance of charm, places to stay and good restaurants. I was greeted on the way in by an eight hundred year old chestnut tree, its location recorded in a treaty signed in the thirteenth century. The tree is also notable for the illusion of a man stepping out of its great gnarled trunk (he could be stepping into the tree also, depending on how the viewer wants to interpret it).

The family-owned Albergue Xacbeo and its bar and restaurant Xacobeo, are excellent examples of the consistent hospitality and well prepared regional cuisine to be found all along the Camino de Santiago. My Sunday dinner that day started with a traditional Gallegan Caldo (soup) of kale, potatoes, leeks and cabbage. The entrée plate was centered with herb roasted potatoes and surrounded with a fan of tender sweet lamb chops, garnished with a splash of chim-churri sauce. The full bottle of house wine was a velvety Bierzo Cabernet Sauvignon—an excellent companion to the lamb. A slice of fresh village cheese with membrillo (a paté of quince jelly) was served with a brandy fortified espresso for dessert. The price for everything was ten Euros. Walking the camino costs less than staying home.

That evening, a tall athletic young man limped into the albergue using a crutch. He spoke to no one and went to bed under a cloud of sadness and pain. His sadness was palpable, an invisible wall, yet it was felt by everyone. The next morning I dressed and went next door for a leisurely breakfast under their flower bedecked arbor. The adventure of a two day side-trip to the ancient monastery of Samos filled my thoughts over coffee.

When I returned to the albergue all the dorms were empty save one bed. The injured young man was still in his mummy shaped sleep sack, zipped closed from head to toe, appearing ever as much as a corpse in the morgue. I could hear no breathing nor could I see the rise and fall of his chest. My greeting got no response, so I resorted to a light tap on his shoulder. He unzipped to expose his face and responded to my concerns in a gracious manner. Grateful for my interest, he showed his swollen injured ankle as evidence for coming down the mountain too fast. He was depressed for having pushed beyond his limits and the possibility of not achieving his goal of atonement and an emotional release at the end of pilgrimage.

My friend's story: His father's recent death left a loss and pain that was unbearable. Alone with grief he decided to walk the camino for closure and time to heal. One week after his father's funeral, his cat was killed and within a few days after that his dog died. He was carrying the ashes of all three to the end of the world—Finesterre, the western most tip of land at the Atlantic Ocean.

When dealing with someone's loss, one way to show compassion is to do something practical for them—show them a map of possibilities that will get them over the immediate roadblocks. The journey to healing is their own. At that point he was unable to see any open roads—they were all blocked. I gave him a short supply of my pain meds and a tube of the same medication in cream form to topically apply to the injury. We went next door for coffee and a reality check.

"This is only an interruption to your plans, it is not a derailment," I told him. "You could take a bus to Sarria. It's a much larger town right on the camino that has all the medical facilities you might need. You can rest there for two or three days. Your ankle will heal in that time and you will continue your pilgrimage wiser and more grateful. You have been slowed down for a reason; take this opportunity to reflect on what that might be. Allow the path to direct your actions by releasing your goals."

We hugged farewell and I left the camino to walk the alternate path to Samos in a happy state of mindfulness and joy. "We practice mindful walking in order to heal ourselves, because walking like that really relieves our worries, the pressure, the tension in our body and our mind." ~ Thich Nhat Hanh

The journey from Triacastela to the fabled Monastery of Samos was only six miles but to stay overnight it was a two day detour from the camino. Even though much of the path skirted a busy highway, it also followed the Oribio River, where the waters provided orchestral background to the constant birdsong. The path was sheltered with old growth hardwoods, bordered with wildflowers and passed over the musical, fast moving river eight times. I lingered at each bridge, watching trout, breathing in the joy and magic as shafts of sunlight created a kaleidoscope of stars on the ripples. Before long, the path took me through a forest, up a mountain and onto a village road where a view opened to the sheltered valley below. It was Samos.

Samos is the largest and the oldest monastery in the western world. The site was first occupied in the first century with a hermitage. It was founded as a monastery in the sixth century by San Martin Dumiense. The enormous square fortress-like complex consumes most of the small valley with the homes and businesses surrounding the exterior walls. The fame and wealth of Samos was so great that during the middle ages it was sacked several times by pirates. In the year 922 King Ordono II brought monks from Aragon to introduce the Benedictine rule—which is still in effect.

In the eleventh century the monastery operated a major hospice for pilgrims to Santiago and continued to expand as kings and royalty flowed their funds, holy gifts and support into its powerbase. In the twelfth century it became part of the Cluny network of abbeys, giving it control of two hundred towns, three hundred monasteries and one hundred five churches. Its fame continued into modern times with forges, farming, schools, herbal pharmacopeia and a library that brought scholars worldwide to its doors.

I followed the river around the walls to the rear where the Benedictines still operate a pilgrims' hostel—sleeping ninety in one long, dormitory room. The clean austere space within the great walls echoed the simple meditative daily lifestyles of services and vespers. After lunch and meditation, one of the monks escorted a few of us on a tour.

The two cloisters were gardens of solitude and peace. The Feijoo Cloister is the largest monastic cloister in Spain—a statue of Father Benito Jeronimo Feijoo y Montenegro sits in the center. Father Feijoo was perhaps Samos's most famous monk (1676-1764), a brilliant student, professor and scientist who lectured widely and published many papers, treatises and books. The Cloister of the Nereidas (nymphs) is a tranquil escape of lush flowering gardens centered round the seventeenth century thirty foot fountain to the Nereidas. Its mighty stone base and upper tiers are supported by life-size marble nymphs.

The sacristy and church are crowned with two sunlit domes in rooms of Baroque splendor. A wedding had taken place before my tour, leaving great urns of white lilies to decorate the altar and entry. Rose petals still covered the aisles. Outside, sunlight streamed through the stone arches of the cloisters to reveal a single monk, elderly and bent over his broom, sweeping errant blossoms back into the garden.

Upstairs above the great cloister, a mural encircles the gallery. It was painted from floor to ceiling and depicts scenes from San Benito's (Saint Benedict's) life. The story unfolds in life size and continues over doorways, windows and niches. At first I was surprised with the modern and simplified cinema backdrop style of art which was in sharp contrast to the architecture around it. These murals were painted in the late 1950s to replace the medieval ones destroyed by fire in 1951. If the graphic paintings are to be believed, Saint Benedict faced many challenges. They include scenes with black robed and hooded monks, apocryphal angels, devils in tights and damsels in peril. Painted over one of the doors—a winged devil is holding a man's head; over another door, three elfish hooded characters read from a book.

Pilgrim activity at the monastery came alive early the next morning as trekkers took to the path at first light. The sun rose in a clear sky promising me a warmer walk than usual. I watched the last of the pilgrims leave from the hostel as I breakfasted on the café patio across the street. At 7:30 the streets were once again deserted as I followed the path around the monastery walls to head west up the mountains.

A German shepherd dog stood guard at the service entrance door, ears up, body ready for action, his attention fully focused on me. I had never had a problem with any dog during my pilgrimage nor did I expect one that day. At the point where the path brought me closest to the doorway, he charged with no sound or warning. By the time I became aware of his movement, he was on me. I had no time to feel fear, no time to react or even to brace myself. The dog threw his body against mine, laid his great head against my chest and stared into my eyes. My hands still held the trekking poles as we stood looking into each other's soul. Satisfied with that encounter of the third kind, he turned and without a sound or tail-wag, resumed the position of guard at the Monastery of Samos.

I knew that I had received a great gift, a confirmation of my state of being. I didn't understand what had happened but I knew how I felt at the moment—it was pure joy and acceptance. As I passed through the hamlet, crossed the river and headed up the mountains I was aware of being consumed by intense happiness. It was beyond any other emotion I had ever encountered.

The path took me around the side of a mountain with lots of shade trees and an occasional farm or meadow. Far below in the valley, my old friend, the Oribio River continued its flow and song as she headed west to join the River Sarria.

The sound of a galloping horse broke the stillness. Spanish pilgrims on horseback were no longer uncommon but to race on narrow wooded paths would endanger both rider and horse. I hurried to get off the trail to the right, where I pushed into the fence that bordered the pasture and waited for them to pass. I turned to face the approaching charge but the sun was at an angle and blinded me. Suddenly I was engulfed in a cloud of dust and a snorting riderless horse that started sniffing my head and upper torso. His reckless affection pushed me off balance and knocked my hat to the ground in the process. I dropped both trekking poles and grabbed onto the fence.

This creature was a spirit of the wind itself. He was a handsome stallion and well groomed. Delicate hooves with white stockings pranced while his flexing muscles rippled under a shiny bay coat—the long flowing red mane and tail caught in the breeze. He came from the upper meadow and stood opposite me, pushing on his side of the fence, his neck resting across my shoulder—inspecting my backpack. With nostrils flaring he passed over my hair, face, and chest as though he were searching for long lost clues as to my identity. I hugged his neck, stroked his flank and imagined the many journeys that we must have shared together.

He came as my friend, bumped my head, smelled of me and caressed me as though to say, "Remember me?" Did we take long moonlight rides back to the Templars Castle after seeing to the safety of pilgrims in peril on the medieval camino? Yes, I felt like we were old friends, longer than time itself. Here we were, once again together; ready to ride off on yet another quest.

For a moment the reality held a great sadness: It was the year 2012, I was an old man walking the camino as a pilgrim myself and he was once again a great stallion tithed and bound to another lord. My memory had been awakened to a time when such a horse nurtured my youth with his affection. I fed deeply on this love that was both ancient and new, real and unreal. We were not animal and man, we were one spirit united in a timeless recognition of being. In our altered state, there was a knowing, that hung like an invisible curtain between the multiverses we now inhabited. I was overjoyed with love for my new friend and imagined the adventures we could have riding together in the forest and along the river.

He stood still, our faces touching each other, our minds whispering of the past, remembering and longing.

He was saying, "Let me take you on another journey, I want nothing more than the freedom to quest together for the noble truths worth fighting for. At the end of each day we can make our beds of sweet smelling hay and have fresh oats from the field and water from the spring for our breakfast." I had read that the way to heaven is on horseback. Was this my mighty steed?

I broke from our reverie, gave my friend a tight hug and returned to walking the camino path. He followed on his side of the fence, matching my pace, until we came to the end of the meadow where the fence stopped at a gate before turning to run up the hillside. He stood at the gate, stomping and snorting as though he might push through or jump over. I returned and embraced his neck, silently sending the message that we were no longer free to choose each other. I had been chosen to walk my pilgrimage alone and that he must be loyal to the lord or lady who cares for him.

"Our love is an old one and it has parted before, but it is not forgotten or lost," I told him. "Besides," I explained, "I will be arrested and put in prison for horse thievery if I take you with me. It is the twenty-first century."

Henry David Thoreau has said, *"Our truest life is when we are in dreams awake."*

The day had given me two incredible encounters with two species of animals. In both cases the communication of love and acceptance was profound and unmistakably demonstrated. I was filled with gratitude and joy as I continued my journey to Sarria. Life is always a gift, whether in a dog, a bird, a cat, a human or a horse. The idea that our life is different or more important than theirs is concocted by man for his own advantage. Animals are great communicators but we must be silent and go within our hearts to learn their language skills. They already know ours.

I had six glorious miles of country path in order to complete the return loop to the main camino and another three miles to the town of Sarria. The wooded path went through many farms and eight small hamlets—each with a few houses grouped around a church, but none had food and beverage services for pilgrims.

A small songbird sitting on a fence sang so intently, that I said "Thank you for that cheerful, sweet song." As I continued walking he flew ahead and once again sat on the fence. As I came abreast, he sang the same song again, only this time much louder.

In Sarria, I had lunch by the river where many had recommended the pulporeria, a restaurant that only serves the famous Pulpo Gallega. I entered a room with five long tables that sat from twelve to twenty persons each. A server carrying several wooden platters of steaming octopus motioned me to find a seat among the many diners. The mood in the room was like a sports bar during a soccer game but there was no TV. It was all about the food—the Pulpo. Two cooks were behind the bar cutting the tentacles from whole boiled octopus into steaming bite sized pieces with scissors. The only choice was for beer or wine, both available from barrels behind the bar. When my octopus was served the server said to cut what I wanted from the loaf of communal two foot rounds of rustic bread. Large rounds of local cheese and loaves of membrillo were left on the tables for dessert, each person hacking out the size portion he wanted. Like most of Galicia, hot coffee laced with local grape skin brandy chases it all down.

19

CONFESSION & COMPASSION

The opposite pole to narcissism is objectivity; it is the faculty to see other people and things as they are, objectively, and to be able to separate this objective picture from a picture which is formed by one's desires and fears.
~Erich Fromm, the Art of Loving

All pilgrims were on count-down to their arrival in Santiago—a mere seventy-one miles down the path. Today's crowd left earlier than usual with plans to walk the fourteen miles to Portomarin—or even further. The crowds were much heavier as we neared the end, making space in official hostels limited. Long queues formed early, making it difficult for families who walked separately to spend their nights together. No one can hold a space for another at official pilgrim hostels. For that reason, hotels and guest houses fill in the gap, but at a much higher price. My days were not goal-driven and I walked less distance than the average—I never met anyone else of any age that had an open schedule to explore as I did.

The walk from Sarria was on beautiful country paths with lots of shade trees, quaint little hamlets and rolling hilly terrain. I walked with a family from Scotland: a couple, the husband, in his early fifties; his wife who was celebrating fifty that day; their daughter, in college studying to be a vet; and the husband's sister, a recent widow in her late sixties. The sister wore her late husband's picture printed on her tee shirt front, and a group picture of her children on the back.

My new friends from Scotland delighted in discussions of local history, farm life along the Camino and Spanish food. "Eat the pulpo," I told them. "It's delicious and never tough and rubbery like in so many places." The sister and I walked at about the same pace allowing the others to move ahead and rest more often.

She wanted to know, "Have you been able to keep up with the Tom Cruise and Katie Holmes split?" She might as well have asked me about the price to ship cargo on a Chinese junk. It seems that the United Kingdom dailies and television had been saturated with front page reporting on the celebrity breakup, with an emphasis on the possible subversive powers of Scientology. How can trivial social conflicts occupy the global press and present it as newsworthy, or as important as global warming or a terrorist attack? Jim Morrison correctly said, "Whoever controls the media—controls the mind."

I had been in Spain for two months with no contact with news reports from any source, including on-line. My children would have contacted me in case of disaster; otherwise I did not want to know. I carried no telephone and relied on e-mail for family communications. I was learning from others how the constant barrage of daily negative reporting impacts our decisions and state of stress. Instant and twenty-four hour global reporting on wars, terrorism, dysfunctional politics, financial crisis, national collapse and mass killings imply that we should know these things.

Going even further, humans are hard wired to care, be helpful and come to our neighbors' rescue. Awareness, coupled with an inability to respond or participate in a solution reduces us to apathetic impudent pawns at the mercy of corporate and doublespeak political manipulators. Our screams of compassion are muffled in the media wilderness—our tribes long disbanded for the sake of the individual.

After eight miles of walking I bid farewell to my Scottish friends and checked into an albergue in the hamlet of Ferreiros, long-famed for its blacksmith traditions, from which its name is derived. Like so many Galician villages, the albergue was in an old converted one-room schoolhouse with just twenty-two bunks. It filled within twenty minutes of opening.

The advantage of staying in remote locations such as Ferreiros allowed me the solitude to meditate, walk the country paths, talk with farmers, and to journal my observations and feelings. I needed time for gratitude and time for reflecting on the miracles of daily encounters. It was empowering to center, to acknowledge and accept the many gifts of guidance that I was receiving. My state of being became motivated through the processing of experiences from the subconscious and spiritual into the conscious awareness of linear time. In other words, through conscious acceptance and gratitude, my new gifts became a functional part of my spiritual toolbox. Once I learned to trust the guidance and empowerment of being in the moment, it became easier to detect subtle energy patterns of resistance and flow.

My decisions had become spontaneous, intuitive choices, not planned and scheduled ones. I did not know in advance where I would stay on any given day. Today, for no reason, Ferreiros became obvious that it was the place, unknown to me the albergue was about to open as I walked up to the building. A group of pilgrims was camped out in the yard waiting. I became the twenty-second person for the twenty-two beds available. Synchronicity, a term coined by Carl Jung, says that we often experience meaningful coincidence that cannot be explained by cause and effect. I had discovered that by accepting the many coincidences that were occurring as meaningful, they were increasing at an exponential rate. They had become part of my guidance system that I started calling *flow*.

After meditation, I went to the only bar and restaurant, a small place whose only call into being was to serve the many pilgrims passing through. The tables were all full but a single lady caught my eye and motioned me to join her.

Eva had stopped on impulse before continuing on to Portomarin. "I wasn't hungry but I would be very hungry if I had waited until the next village. Perhaps I was supposed to have dinner with you," she stated, as though she knew that I would understand the implications intended.

"I don't consider this opportunity for us to meet a coincidence at all. This must be the right place and right time for our friendship and to share our journeys," I assured her.

Eva had been divorced for several years and had decided that married life was not the answer for her. She longed to experience life at a more meaningful level, but didn't know how to get there. She had tried several religious pathways with no results other than being part of the community. She had seen the movie *The Way* and immediately felt that the camino would, "at least give me some clues for my own path."

"I started in St. Jean Pied De Port with the enthusiasm of the running of the bulls, but the mountains took their toll on my feet and legs; by the third day I had to seek medical help." She continued, "After two days of rest, I slowed down and have met some wonderful people, made many friends, and have learned so much about the history. It's amazing how much of Spain's history is connected to all of us, especially the Americas and Europe."

I agreed that the enthusiasm of discovery could awaken us to more treasures within and would continue, as long as we maintained the search to excavate our feelings and accept the truth. "Of course, there are always doubts, obstacles and fears that would like to distract us from becoming fully human," I offered. "We need to trust our intuitive guidance system and realize that our lives are not regulated by random coincidences, to be passed off as mere chance of cause and effect."

Eva's spoon of soup became suspended midair, her face beaming into a full smile. Eyes locked on mine she exclaimed, "Yes! We are so much more than what we have been told. We are not only greater than the sum of the parts; we can become empowered by the synergistic relationship of accepting and sharing our truth with others. The flow of synchronicity will provide all opportunities necessary to confirm the beings of light and wisdom that we are becoming. We only have to avoid the temptation to explain it away."

A magical fog swirled around the tiny hamlet of Ferreiros as I prepared for the next day's journey. It seemed to select certain buildings for obscurity while others were revealed as though rendered in life size-sepia photographs. The next six miles skirted the mountain crest before making a steep descent at Portomarin, a town worthy of exploration.

Talking With Cats

Located in the deep Mino Valley on the river of the same name, Portomarin has had a bridge for east-west passage since Roman times. It has been destroyed and replaced by every invading culture and war since then. In the 1950s the government constructed a dam on the river to provide hydroelectricity for the region. Most of the town's historic buildings had to be moved, stone by stone, to higher ground on the western bank. The remainder of the medieval town lies at the bottom of the new body of water. Locals say that when the water table is low, the old town appears—like a ghost from the past.

I crossed the new iron bridge and climbed the old stone stairs into the new town. The town is amazing in its reconstruction; the busy stone-covered Main Street, Rua Xeral Franco, climbs towards the Plaza Major with massive stone colonnades on both sides. The wide sheltered arcades were active with restaurants, bars, grocers, and all services.

Standing in the center of the cobblestone plaza, the austere church of San Nicolas rises like a great monolith. Every stone had to be removed, numbered and carried up the hill for reassembly. In the twelfth century it was the church and fortress of The Knights of Saint John. The top is crowned with battlements that join four corner towers adding drama to the tall straight—sided building. Recessed above the great arched entry is a heroic-sized rose window. It is the largest in width and height, single-nave Romanesque church in Galicia. The church and new town are as much a testament to the stonemasons that rebuilt them, as to the ones of the twelfth century who created them.

I was warmly greeted by Manuel at his small albergue, where my backpack had arrived earlier. Manuel and his wife operate their clean, sixteen-bed hostel with all the hospitality and care one would expect at home. The kitchen is cozy, but large enough to accommodate several tables where we pilgrims lingered and shared stories late into the evening. Ramon and Jules, two young cyclists from France, were curious how I had received so many stamps in my pilgrim's passport.

"Walk slowly and visit lots of historical monuments and churches," I told them.

They would complete seven hundred eighty miles in two weeks and arrive in Santiago the next night. "We haven't had much time to see anything. We make sandwiches every night to eat on the road so we don't have to stop," Ramon told me. "Our passports will have barely enough stamps to qualify for a Compostela," Jules said.

Earlier, I had attended a concert hosted by the city of Portomarin for all pilgrims in town that evening. The event was held in the church of San Nicolas, which has a greeter in the reception area to assist pilgrims with questions, lodging, and to stamp their passport. The concert featured the extraordinary talent of a young man who performed on guitar, flute and voice. His program included selections by Bach, Marais and Telemann. The vocal portion featured early Spanish cantos and Sufi laments.

The excitement in the plaza outside, in the bars and restaurants, and on the camino continued to build daily as we approached Santiago and Saint James Day on July twenty-fifth. For me, there were only fifty-eight miles and five days to go. Many others would complete the trek in two days.

A social worker from Germany joined me while I was recording my thoughts and events of the day in my journal.

"Pardon me, may I sit with you? You seem to be someone that I can talk with," she said.

"Of course, my best teachers are among those who have time to talk and share their experiences," I replied.

Fran had a lot she wanted to talk about but what flowed most easily were her walking experiences, blisters, observations and more specifically, her three walking companions. "They are really nice ladies but they want me to do everything they do with them. I've left them twice, making excuses to be alone, but as luck would have it, they have found me each time," she said.

"Did you arrive in Spain with these ladies, and have you told them that you prefer to walk alone?" I asked.

"No, we met in Leon and I actually enjoyed their company for a few days. It's just when I wanted to walk alone that they begged me to stay and kept telling me how much they enjoyed my friendship. One of them wants to mother me; she is constantly giving me advice and even chooses what food I should eat. Everything is on their schedule—where we stay and when we eat. I'm starting to feel like I'm in prison," she blurted out.

Talking With Cats

"It's your challenge if you want to end their domination and control," I suggested. "Be firm but considerate when you say that you came to the camino on a personal pilgrimage to be alone. Thank them for their friendship but "I think you should refuse all offers to meet again, whether it's in Santiago, on the coast or in your hometown."

"I left them today, but I know they will be waiting for me along the road tomorrow. I was considering staying here an extra day to avoid the confrontation," Fran said.

"No, from my experience, this is a teaching that you need to learn. It may be directly connected to why you are here walking the camino. Confront this fear and break their control over you," I felt impassioned to say.

"My own pilgrimage has been bringing the teaching that I am ready for." I told her. Whether you know it or not, everything is unfolding as it should. Maybe not as you may have imagined, but you arrived on this path open to solutions—here they are, I said.

I think you're ready to deal with control issues or they would not have come in such obvious and clear form. You will be proud and grateful to discover your inner strength to solve this problem."

Tears started to flow as she reached for my hand. "Thank you for letting me talk; I know this is an old issue. My mother controlled my life, she chose my profession, and destroyed both my marriages. I actually came to the camino to escape her domination and to find myself," Fran said.

"Wow, what a gift your three friends have provided—through them, you have come to recognize not only the truth of the situation, but the opportunity to bring about a solution. I suspect that once you confront the oppressors down the road, many other solutions will come before you return to Germany," I said. "In releasing yourself from bondage, you will also release your mother. She loves you so much she's afraid she will lose you if she doesn't control you," I assured her. "I'm happy that you came to talk with me, just an old pilgrim walking the path, in search of his own truth. Your openness and candor shows that you're well on the way to heal and find happiness. I'm learning that the solutions we seek in life are within us all along. I'm glad you could release yours."

W. Lee Nichols

    We all have ghosts and shadows from the past that want to walk with us. I marveled at how the simple act of walking alone can expose the presence of dark specters and put light on solutions to become free of them. Like the medieval knights who confronted their fears, we all must summon the courage to challenge ours. The reward is the freedom to live a meaningful life full of acceptance, love, and the awareness of being at one with the world.

20

THE INNER CHILD

In every real man a child is hidden that wants to play.
~Friedrich Nietzsche

Solitude on the camino was no longer an option. The mood was festive with more and more small groups jousting for space to stay abreast of each other. At all times during today's eight mile walk, at least ten other pilgrims were in sight—a major adjustment for those of us who had been alone for several hours every day, for over four hundred miles. Some older individuals disliked the festive mood of laughter and playful games of chase, and running past others to catch up. I loved the new excitement, having taken the attitude that everyone had the right to express themselves, differently perhaps, but as valid as my own choices.

At one time, a group of teenagers skipped past me, but one of them lagged behind, continuing to walk. The others started to tease him for not being able to skip. "Come on, I'll show you how," I offered.

You can imagine the group's delight and laughter at seeing a seventy-two year old man skipping down the mountain path, large cotton hat flopping, trekking poles held aloft, looking ever so much like a booby bird learning to fly. After that outrageous display, the young man was no longer afraid to try, and caught up with his friends.

To benefit most on the camino, we can't allow judgments and personal expectations to take us out of our own joy and state of being in the moment. We can become wise compassionate observers, which often leads to our best teachers. Every day on the Way of Saint James presented new circumstances for growth and discovery. Welcome to the laboratory called life, I thought.

I arrived in Gonzar to find the roadside bar and restaurant overflowing into the street as perhaps eighty to one hundred pilgrims snacked, used the bathroom, and visited with each other. At all times, a constant flow of newcomers were replacing an equal flow of departures. During the last one hundred kilometers (sixty miles) pilgrims must obtain at least two stamps in their passport every day. The Café Descanso Del Peregrino in Gonzar was an official location for the stamp.

The camino normally joined the connecting highways in each village, entering and departing outside of the towns to once again become a walking trail through rural countryside. In Gonzar, taxis were cruising through very slowly, often stopping just before or after the village center. They were trolling for weak, tired or injured pilgrims to take them "almost" to their desired stop. The rules for walking the camino, for staying in official hostels and to receive the hostels stamp on our passport, states that we cannot arrive by vehicle. For that reason, those who either cannot or will not play by the rules, use the taxi service to the edge of town—where they get out and walk the remaining distance.

For those like myself, who have walked the entire camino, a few exceptions to the rule early on would be no problem, but during the final one hundred kilometers abuse is frowned upon for everyone. There are no camino police, just the conscience of the good people who walk it, who must answer this question asked at the Cathedral in Santiago: "Did you walk the last one hundred kilometers (two hundred for bicycle) of the camino?"

The wisdom of the path and the feedback from my body told me that Ventas de Naron would be home for that night. Two of the stone farmhouses were operated as hostels, each with its own restaurant. Casa

Molar was an excellent personal choice with just eighteen bunks and a few private rooms on the second floor. The houses and barns of the village were divided by stone walls, which also lined the country lanes and enclosed grazing sheep or lush gardens filled with greens, lettuces, potatoes and tomatoes.

After a shower and a home cooked meal of Gallegan kale soup and stew, I walked up a farm path, climbed across the fence, and entered a dense pine forest with thick beds of fresh aromatic needles underfoot. I found a spot where shafts of bright sunlight filtered down through the canopy, projecting a moving picture in shadows on the forest floor as the wind gently swayed the upper branches.

I sat down to reflect and meditate with my back resting against the trunk of a tall pine, which had his own tale to tell—I was there to listen. My mind struggled to understand the joy that I was experiencing, as the inner child merged with consciousness to become whole again. A memory flooded my senses. When I was a troubled ten-year-old boy, I rode my horse to such a place and found similar sanctuary and peace. I quit struggling to understand; the breeze whispered, "Release, let go, just be here and know that you are loved."

"The lover of nature is he whose inward and outward senses are still adjusted to each other; who has retained the spirit of infancy even into the era of manhood."—Ralph Waldo Emerson.

We awoke into a world of total whiteout. The dense fog held the little village captive, but not for my fellow pilgrims. Most left in darkness and fog; searching their way with flashlights, while fears of having no place to stay that night became their motivator and guide. I lingered at the bar that morning where the friendly staff prepared breakfast and shared stories of village and farm life. The walk to Palas De Rei (Palace of the King) was on a beautiful natural trail through woodlands and hillside. I wanted it all to myself.

A full mile before entering the village, modern accommodations, hostels and lodges lined the camino. One of the hostels had been tagged as a Pavilion Palas de Rei. A circus of vendors, government agencies and camino friends were on hand ready to stamp passports and offer support or medical attention. Hundreds of pilgrims stood in lines for their services and advice as to where they might find a bed.

It was Saturday and the village was in the midst of market day. I had sent my backpack ahead to a hostel that I knew was near the Romanesque Church of San Tirso, which I thought would be easy to find. Normally, I suppose it would be, but the market of hanging tapestries, tents and fruits and vegetables obscured the view and even the patterns of streets and plazas. It took many helpful citizens to guide me to my lodging. Along the way every hostel had long lines of pilgrims that would more than fill each of them. My chosen location had received my backpack, but they too had filled. "It is the busiest week of the year," the owner told me. "With just three days until the celebration of Saint James Day there are no places available between here and Santiago."

This was the first time not to have my choice of albergue immediately confirmed. I avoided becoming concerned, assuming that this was an opportunity to open to trust and allow flow to guide me. I had learned that obstacles only remained obstacles as long as I saw them as such. In my thoughts, I was being guided to a location that would be removed from the congested hostels, in which some were placing mattresses on the floor for overflow. Something or some thought had guided me to choose a site near the San Tirso church; perhaps I should go there.

I pushed my way through the crowds to the church plaza with the intention of going inside to meditate and wait for a solution. As I stood contemplating the beauty of the church's great Romanesque façade, a gentleman interrupted my reverie. "Buenos dias señor, may I be of assistance?" he asked. "I know a friend who rents rooms. Let's walk over there and see if she has any left." He took me by the arm to a nearby café where the owners had remodeled their home that spring, and had four modern, well equipped private rooms with bath. The house sat to the back of the café on a small private courtyard. One room was available for twenty Euros. Once he had been assured that I had a room, my kind guide disappeared back into the crowd before I could extend my thanks.

Earlier, I had seen a pulporeria with crowds in front that were watching the open-kitchen preparation of the regional delicacy. I went back to investigate and sample the reason for its popularity. Without my backpack and trekking poles, it was easier to get close to the window and see the show.

Directly in front of the window was a small open room surrounded by a counter on the interior. About twenty long tables, which seated twelve diners each, filled the large and narrow dining room. A bar ran from the front door down the room's left side. But the action was in the window. Two very large, bubbling cauldrons stood waist high in the center, with a ring of gas fire incorporated in the base of each. Crates of large octopus with foot-long tentacles were lowered and retrieved from the cauldrons with long meat hooks. A matronly, grey-haired woman held court over the cauldrons, with two assistants. Their tools were large scissors. The steaming octopus was held in their gloved left hands while they snipped rings of tender meat from the tentacles onto an assembly of wooden plates lined down the counter. One of the assistants' drizzled olive oil and sprinkled seasoned red pepper on the steaming plates as servers rushed them off to drooling aficionados.

I found a seat at one of the long tables and the vigilant staff brought bread and wine. "We have fresh pimentos de Pardon today," one told me. These are peppers so delicious they are worth a plane ticket to Spain. They are grown in the area around the small village of Pardon, not far off the camino in Galicia. The thumb-sized peppers are always deep fried in olive oil and sprinkled with sea salt. Unlike jalapenos and many other peppers, the pimentos de Pardon have thin skins that do not require peeling. Their flavor is sweet and delicate, with a hint of chili poblano flavor, but they are not hot. They are eaten whole as an appetizer or side dish. I was told that the production is so small that none are exported.

One of life's great pleasures is the joy of delicious, fresh food that has been well-prepared in the simplest manner. The tender pulpo and sweet peppers were outstanding examples of fine culinary discipline. On the way out I stopped to speak with the doña and thank her for the great meal. "How many kilos of pulpo do you serve?" I asked. "Most of the year we use about two hundred kilos every day," she told me. At that rate, multiplied by the hundreds of restaurants that serve it, delicious as it is, octopus will soon become another species harvested into extinction. I am aware that Spain's consumption may well be far below that of most Asian cultures where the growing demand for seafood has seriously threatened many species. Globally, all food sources in the twenty-first century will require reexamining where some finite supplies cannot remain sustainable without conservation efforts. I would like to imagine that my grandchildren and their descendants will also be able to enjoy the same delicious meal that I had.

The camino no longer offered an opportunity for meditation, reflection or personal space. Now, those arts must be carried within our hearts, having learned them during earlier days when solitude was a given. Like water, a reserve of compassion and acceptance sustains us. We had new tests and lessons to learn: how to co-exist with fellow humans under stressful, crowded conditions. The security and confidence that the camino had been teaching me was humbling—I did not have to participate in the struggle. A much greater force was guiding my steps, making my choices, and giving me the wisdom to experience the joy of being in the moment.

The path out of Palas de Rei flowed through cool canopied forests, over several river beds, around hillsides and several villages on the way to Melide. We crossed and re-crossed the busy highway several times; fortunately it did not dog our path. Pilgrims walked side-by-side with little space in-between as the endless migration snaked its way westward. The mood was festive with animated talk and laughter erupting among the many groups.

New friendships sprang up which frequently rearranged the walking patterns: teen girls gossiped, giggled and gasped in awe as each took turns revealing star-struck secrets. Teen boys could not be contained—they jogged, skipped, ran and played games in the woods. The parents formed their own cliques, usually in small groups of men discussing sports, and women swapping stories of children and social issues. Finally, in the group category, were church and school tours comprised of mixed teens that were herded in flocks of twenty to thirty.

The elderly and single pilgrims were the outsiders as they struggled for space and footing among the faster moving groups. Finding a place to urinate in private became a challenge of immense proportions, especially for women. Most men became talented at pretending to be adjusting their backpack and clothing while partially hidden behind a tree or clump of bushes. A backpack, trekking poles and a clutter of outer clothing piled on the ground usually meant that a woman was nearby, so find another tree. The groups had it easier: they simply built human walls of protection, facing the path, as though nothing was going on behind their back. It began to look like a summer snowfall as tissue littered the forest floor—a visual disaster for the path—a warning to the rest of us.

Melide, a town of some eight thousand, is surrounded with numerous Neolithic dolmens that attest to its prehistoric past. Once again, I arrived in a town that was sold out—there were no beds available. I toured the church museum and asked the caretaker what my options might be—perhaps the parish could provide a space on their floor. He escorted me to an unmarked building, where a new pension provided five-star accommodations within my meager budget.

Most pilgrims were going to walk to Santiago the next day in one trek of thirty-five miles. The flow to reach Santiago in time for the festival was pulling me faster than I had imagined or wanted to go. But perhaps that was the master plan; to remain in the flow and offer no resistance. The message was becoming clear; for some reason, I knew that I was supposed to be in Santiago for Saint James Day—but how?

I discussed all possibilities with the pension owner's son, Pablo. I was not willing to walk the entire distance in one day, but could divide it into two, allowing for my arrival on festival eve. We looked over my camino map and decided that the small village of Salceda would be a good midpoint to rest overnight. Pablo called a private resort that he knew and secured a confirmed reservation. They were booked full with private tours; but just today, one of the groups had canceled a room for the next night. The more I stepped out of the way and allowed the natural progression of flow to carry me forward, the more magical the pilgrimage became.

I went out to celebrate the gifts that I had been receiving, the joy of discovery and the empowerment of awareness. Today, I was hungry for a steak—it would be my first on the Camino. Pablo recommended that I visit the popular pulporeria where they were also known for charcoal steaks. A mug of Galician Estrella beer and a platter of pimentos Pardon were only bested with a local T-bone steak that was marbled and cooked to juicy perfection. Sometimes the primal carnivore needs to be fed.

21

MARCH TO GLORY

*To walk safely through the maze of human life, one needs
the light of wisdom and the guidance of virtue.*
~Buddha

It was not a festive day on The Camino de Santiago, especially here at the final stage. The number of pilgrims was as heavy as the day before, but their body language had changed. Gone were the gaiety, laughter and animated conversations. Today, it was eyes forward, strides longer and a determined set in their jaws as bodies lock-stepped in a mindless march. The collective language was "move faster, see less and don't let anyone get ahead of you." It was a human, walking version of traffic on the Los Angeles freeway.

I withdrew to a village café where empanadas, donuts and coffee became fuel for the climb up a small mountain to the village of Arzùa. I reflected on fellow pilgrims at early stages of the camino versus their conduct during the final few days. Earlier, there had been an open enthusiasm for every meadow of flowers, every monument and every church and mountain waterfall. There was compassion for each other's wounds and needs as well as a friendly greeting along the way. On the camino it is easy to see how quickly we can revert to our old selves when challenged with familiar stress conditions.

Today, the principal topics of conversation were the hour of expected arrival, the rudeness of fellow pilgrims, the size of the crowds, shortage of accommodations, and the sudden heat spell. One chap from London, who had already walked over eight hundred miles, exclaimed, "what has happened to our camino?" It seemed to me that what had happened was that the observer had changed what he chose to see; the Sphinx stands silent, waiting as always, to reveal her riddles. The Way, like the Sphinx, is a buffet of mysteries, wisdom, truth, love, beauty and acceptance. It also offers an equal smorgasbord of fear, distrust, judgments, stress, suffering and pain. It is revealing to see what we put on our plate.

The Posada in Salceda was a modern construction of low-slung stone buildings decorated with a swimming pool and waterfall. It was not in the village proper and operated with an all-inclusive price with services designed for the tour groups that it was built to accommodate. The owners were gracious and allowed me to pay à la carte for the single meal that I required. The quiet, remote setting was wonderful for doing the domestic chores of laundry and meditating. At sunset I explored the small town, farms and paths that would connect me to the camino through the forest the next day. I expected to leave at five in the morning and the traditional trail marks would be difficult to find in full darkness.

Late that evening I stopped in a grove of trees that sheltered a hidden clearing of grass and stone. Here, trees and the dusty path melted away into darkness while the stars filled the center with dazzling brightness. I was drawn to stay, take a position on a slab of stone, and contemplate the force that was guiding every step and decision of my pilgrimage. What door had I opened, what switch had I flipped on to allow me to be in this state of grace and happiness? I was humbled and grateful; aware that my path had been liberated from suffering, my doubts transformed into acceptance, and most of all, the floodgates to my past had been opened and released.

I was looking for a fresh new language to express my feelings and the empowerment that lifted my pilgrimage to a new level of being. Had I been chosen or had I chosen? It was too late to ignore or deny the new dimension of awareness that I now walked in. My state of being was one that fears had always locked me out of before, even though in reflection, I now realized that there had always been guides and doorways waiting for me. Why had I refused to open those doors until now? Was it ego fed by fear? Fear of accepting the empowerment, the wisdom, the light of being a small creature in an infinite universe. One unchained by dogma and hypocrisy.

I suspect that all souls are standing near the doorway that leads to their own freedom and truth. To find that door requires courage and the curiosity to search for it. Often the key to unlock our prison door has also been hidden, but clues or riddles will lead us to it if we pass their test. For me, the camino had provided the privacy and time to find my key and to accept the subtle guidance that is always present in our lives.

The crucible for change can occur anywhere and anytime; our job is to prepare for that journey when it does arrive. It will often arrive in a cloud of chaos, confusion and personal upheaval which will reduce the old demons into whimpering puppies in comparison. Without being conscious of what I was doing, I had opened the door to transformation when I accepted the atonement of who I had been during the few days spent in Madrid. I had already suffered the chaos of loss; next, I had to wipe the slate clean. I confessed to my conscious self the many masks and deceits of my past, with the desire to become whole and transparent. I was willing to dump the trash of illusion and to welcome an infusion of light and freedom. With that simple open invitation from me, the camino said, "Come and get it, we are ready for you."

There is another unspoken force in this story: as I explore my own awakening and pathway to discovery, I suspect that the clue is literally right under my nose. Its name is "Walking." Our western culture has rid itself of ritual and the need of rites of passage. Within all early cultures, rites of passage celebrated birth, adolescence, achievements and elevation into social groups, marriage and death. Some of the celebrations could last years, but all involved actions and/or commitments, which suggested a new state-of-being on an infinite spiral of becoming. Walking to a sacred place or in a certain pattern that suggested transcendence of space and time was often involved in most early ritual.

In his marvelous 1986 book, *Songlines*, Bruce Chatwin tells the Australian Aboriginal creation myth of how their people sang themselves into existence. They walked the barren featureless landscape and sang every feature of the natural world into existence. As the people walked and sang of animals, rivers, trees, rocks and grasses, those things sprang into being and flourished. Every generation since has taken its babies on its backs and walked the land, singing the maps of territory and identity, plant by plant, rock by rock. Chatwin concluded that the majority of human history took place walking.

Throughout the millennia, humans have walked on great pilgrimages such as during the Crusades to Jerusalem or Santiago, to the sacred Ganges in India, or to Mecca in Saudi Arabia. For over a thousand years hermits wandered the earth on foot in search of their gods. Longer still, nomadic tribes have carried the seeds of their culture and earth-teachings to every corner of our planet. And they did it walking.

Like the spiral double helix of our DNA, life does not unfold in a linear pattern. We are not born as whole creatures ready to feed and turn loose without having some type of map to find our way. Those maps are encoded within us and need to be awakened to become functional. To break the code, we must find the key. Animals instinctly understand the required rituals to initiate and awaken their young into responsible models of the species. We humans have long dismissed the rituals of tribal life that once awakened our youth to become whole and aware of a shared journey.

Walking may well be the key to open one of the most primal codes locked deep within us. From my own experience, several days must be spent walking to nurture the bud and foster its development into full bloom. Once the bloom appears, we awaken to an awareness of our place in the pantheon of life's ever evolving spiral of being. After awakening, a normal hour or two of regular walking discipline will continue to nourish and encourage multiple blooms of awareness and a sense of well-being. In this state we begin our journey at one with all life. Happiness springs from the knowing, and that can only come from within. My pilgrimage has taught that once we take our position in the flow of the universe, we are held aloft by its sheer energy and rewarded with its warm embrace of love, wisdom and guidance.

I left my backpack to be shipped forward via taxi in order to walk the fifteen miles to Santiago unencumbered. There was no moon and the barns and trees traced only a vague black outline on a somber window of sky when I left the posada at five-thirty a.m. In order to get back to the camino proper I had to trek on farm roads that were bordered with old growth hardwoods. The path was totally invisible. Fortunately, I had walked it the previous evening and remembered helpful details.

During long journeys, we fall into routines of discipline as we prepare for the next day's travel. Laundry, folding and packing become a mindless process with canteen, toothbrush and a fresh change of clothing laid out and waiting. Today had lots of exceptions for error in preparation. The big one became evident the moment I entered total darkness; I had left my flashlight in the shipped backpack. Even though the winding farm-path was wide enough for a tractor, I had difficulty staying within its parameters, often stumbling into the weeds and bushes. Eventually, the path straightened and the dim sky became a grey notch between the tree lines to follow.

Despite this difficulty I felt exhilarated and happy to be in the cool morning stillness. I crossed the empty highway, passed between the few shuttered buildings, and found the trail marker, which immediately directed me into another forest. Galicia has installed concrete trail markers every kilometer during the last one hundred km of the camino. It helps pilgrims to observe their progress, stay on the path and build enthusiasm for arrival in Santiago. Each one stands about three feet high with a diameter of six inches and an embossed shell of Santiago at the top. The actual km number is either embossed or lettered into the side of the column. At some stage near the end, the columns start appearing more frequently, even every tenth of km, especially when the path has deviations for farm roads and highway crossings. In the dark forest that morning, those markers became my only guide.

At six-thirty I was still in the dark and making slow progress, using my trekking poles like a blind man's cane to stay out of the trees. In the distance, a faint light became a guiding star. It was an exposed low wattage light bulb attached to a barn beside the path. Thanks to the light, I soon discovered from my maps that the camino crisscrossed the highway to Santiago on several occasions. At the next crossing I took to the highway, following the white line west. I was alone; there were no pilgrims and there was no traffic. When daylight came it would be easy to take up the sacred path again.

A rose-colored dawn ushered in a new day as I picked up the path that flowed through heavily forested country, with small hills and a beautiful river at the village of Arca. Soon I arrived in the industrial complex that surrounds one of Santiago's three major airports, Lavacolla.

There was an eerie solitude on the camino. During the first five miles I encountered just eight other pilgrims. Even in Lavacolla, there were no large groups and often I would not be within sight of another person. Tonight, on the eve of Santiago's Feast Day, the festival would begin with fireworks and musical venues to entertain the assembled masses. I had expected the mindless march to continue into today. Not so. For most, the lack of beds had dictated thirty-five mile walks and an early arrival. No one was willing to arrive with no place to stay, except me.

It must have required co-operative planning from the developers at the huge Lavacolla International Airport, highway officials and regional government to wind the camino through the airport complex without cultural shock. The path remained on tree-shaded dirt with frequent streams of clear water, babbling waterfalls and songbirds. The airport runways, terminals and hangars were on elevated, fenced ground just thirty feet above the tranquil path—a fact most pilgrims are unaware of, until an incoming flight ruffles their hair. I was amazed when a rabbit crossed my path, unafraid and unhurried, stopping to rest in a patch of wildflowers nearby.

West of the airport, the path begins a moderate to steep climb that continues for three miles until it reaches the top at Monte de Gozo. The Mountain of Joy was so named because of the euphoria experienced by early pilgrims when they first saw the spires of the Cathedral of Santiago. Even though the city lies in a valley three more miles to the west, the great spires remain visible above the old, walled hill-top town, now surrounded with a large bustling modern city.

Monte de Gozo has recently been crowned with an enormous bronze sculpture commemorating the 1993 holy year when the pope visited. The last mile of the road at the peak is lined with vendors, bars, restaurants and a giddy atmosphere where friends and family unite, take pictures and share a celebratory glass of wine before the final thrust into the city. I arrived after the fact. Most everyone had arrived and gone into Santiago yesterday.

Huddled against the western side of the mountain, a mere one hundred yards from the top, is the modern campus complex of dormitories for pilgrims called Albergue Monte de Gozo. A maze of twenty dormitories housing fifty each, stair-step down the mountain on landscaped grounds with courtyards, cafeterias, laundromats, bars, restaurants and all services needed to recover from a five hundred mile walk. For me, this was a wise choice for a place to stay since most everyone else wanted to be in the sold-out city.

I was assigned to one of the rooms accommodating four persons and went to collect my backpack from the reception.

"We don't accept backpacks from the courier services," the clerk told me. "Normally, we house over five hundred pilgrims and we are not staffed to receive and distribute their belongings. Nor do we have the space to adequately handle the security and storage of so many bags."

"Then, where would my bag have been sent?" I inquired.

"Try asking at some of the bars at the top of the hill. That's as far as the taxis go," I was politely informed.

It was at the third bar from the top. It was not the only one either, as the bartender showed me a closet stuffed with backpacks.

"Some people never come to collect their bags," he said. "They buy all new things and a suitcase in Santiago. They never want to see the old dirty, sweaty things that have barely survived the long walk."

That was not my story, I had a long journey left after Santiago and I was pleased to have my support team back in hand. I had a few potential obstacles to overcome in order to participate in festival activities during the next two days. I took them to the hospitalero of Monte de Gozo.

I told them I'd like to go into the city and attend the celebrations tonight, but I couldn't get back by the curfew time of eleven p.m. I also wanted to attend all of the highlights of tomorrow's program, but wouldn't have time to search for a room, and couldn't carry a backpack to the restricted, high security events. Of lesser importance, I asked if there is any mode of transportation available. One of the best lessons that I had received on the entire pilgrimage was not to assume that there would be problems. I had a vision in mind that needed the input from someone who had the authority to make it happen. And he did.

"Please go tonight, and stay for our famous La Fachada firework display at midnight. When you return, I will leave the back door unlocked. Tomorrow, make your bed and leave your backpack on top with your name attached and sir, please consider that an invitation to stay with us tomorrow night, he said. On the following day there will be plenty of rooms in the city. These two days are official holidays and we have over one million pilgrims and tourists in town to celebrate. Transportation is unable to move through the city. Buses and taxis will be rare and only on the periphery." He smiled, took my hand and said, "I am glad to help you any way that I can, but unfortunately you will have to walk into the city and back tonight. We hope your stay in Santiago will bring you great joy and happiness, may God bless you."

I walked the three miles feeling happy to have been caught up in the flow and magic of one of Europe's oldest and most festive celebrations. Even my feet and legs were strong and happy to participate in the euphoria of the day. I thanked them for the first fifteen miles that morning, and now they were energized and ready to go again.

Santiago is beautiful the way Rome and Paris are. It was built on a hill, for drama if nothing else, a stage on many levels to give each of the actors an opportunity for the spotlight. Wide cobblestone streets connect plaza to plaza and monuments to fountains. They lead through arcaded walks and under arches spanning Romanesque palaces. The town is a candy store of visual treats. Of course, all streets go to the great Obradoiro Square where the twin spires of the cathedral rise to meet the sky. The handsome, great square can accommodate fifty thousand celebrants.

During my tour of the town I happened upon the cathedral's official Pilgrims' office where I presented myself to receive the Compostela, the certificate acknowledging completion of my pilgrimage to Santiago.

When I departed, a wave of sadness flashed over me. "I don't want it to end," I thought. Of course it wasn't going to end yet; I had a few more weeks for the pilgrimage to guide me further on this magical journey. I had no idea where that might be, but the camino continued on to Finisterre and Muxia on the Atlantic coast. The end of the known world might be a good place to start.

22

LA FACHADA

*Your time is limited, so don't waste it living someone else's life.
Don't be trapped by dogma—which is living
with the results of other people's thinking.*
~ Steve Jobs

Last night the city was filled with stages of live music hosting International headliners, an orchestra in the square, small musical ensembles on plazas, a harp trio, and a solo violinist. Numerous bagpipers also brought the ancient tunes of the Galician Celts to the streets. At ten p.m., the police started crowd control on Obradoiro Square, as preparations were made for the midnight show that everyone came for. When it was full, they sealed the gates for the safety of those inside. Now, we would see one of Europe's most spectacular displays of projection, laser and pyrotechnics called *La Fachada*.

When projection technology is combined with skilled editing and the creative use of traditional fireworks and laser, the illusions they create are breathtaking. At one point the cathedral collapsed, stone by stone into the great square. Like the Phoenix, it rose again only to be reclaimed with vines and exotic foliage curling up the façade, around the portals and to the top of the great towers.

Later, the police helped me through the crowds and to find the street that would lead to the highway, and the three-mile-walk back to Monte de Gozo. The city continued to party until daybreak. I arrived in my room at two-thirty in the morning, exhilarated and happy beyond comprehension. My body was electric with energy and ready for more. I felt like the stamina of my youth had returned to empower every cell into action.

The time for more came before the first glow of morning crested the horizon. I showered, dressed and began the three-mile-hike back for the somber ceremonies that would celebrate the Feast Day of Santiago. The morning's event was split between two connecting venues: the cathedral and Obradoiro Square.

At nine a.m., I had to choose which ceremony and location to watch. The cathedral would host a mass at ten for a standing-room-only audience. A procession of dozens of elegantly robed and caped clergy, bishops and Knights of Santiago would then exit down the double baroque staircase, and cross the red carpeted square to receive the Spanish King and noble guests. After formalities, the procession reversed itself, with nobles in tow, and returned to the Apostle at the Feast Mass to Santiago in the cathedral.

I chose to be inside where I could witness the ceremony using the giant, six foot, fourteenth-century censor called the *Botafumeiro*. Ostensibly, it was designed to camouflage the offensive odors rising from the medieval crowds of un-bathed pilgrims. Regardless, the sterling silver censor is loaded with enough smoking incense to set off most fire alarms. Eight red-robed monks each hold cords connecting to a master rope looped through a pulley attached to the ceiling, one hundred feet above the crowd. Once the fiery Botafumeiro is set in motion, it sails out over the crowds to the Hymn of Santiago played on the church's mighty organ. The clouds of exotic and aromatic incense settle over the worshippers and all but obscure the monks heaving on the great rope.

I love ceremony and ritual. I think it is unfortunate that modern sophistication has denuded us of magical realism and mythical transcendence. We don't need to understand or have a printed explanatory text to everything we do. Letting go with trust, without conscious understanding of an event or ceremony, can leave us to wonder, and it transports us to realms of awareness never experienced before. Our imagination goes beyond conscious knowledge and convention—if we let it.

The next day I left Monte de Gozo with a couple of pilgrims from Barcelona to take up residence in Santiago for four days. They had a hotel reservation and I was going to walk the hillside around the cathedral in search of a reasonable hostal or pension. I felt guided to follow my instincts and let the flow continue to show me the way. Fortunately, city buses were now running and one appeared within five minutes of our descent from the mountain. We had coffee and crescents in town before parting to find lodging.

I walked to the highest part of the old town where a large plaza overlooked the cathedral, the countryside to the west, and the sprawling modern city to the east. With that perspective in focus, I entered into a complex maze of small cobblestone streets where merchants, tradesmen, bakeries and bookstores occupied Baroque, Romanesque and Gothic structures, each an architectural wonder.

I wanted to get lost; to have no reference or conscious guide to refer to. It was an opportunity to trust the guidance that had befriended me on the camino. At each intersection, I stopped, waited and looked—not down the street, but within, for some feeling, some 'aha' of awareness. Soon I was staring at a small, oval, metal sign with classic but ornate lettering. It hung over the narrow street on a brick building with French doors on the second level. I had to get closer to read what the small lettering said. Pazo de Agra Hostal had one room, priced within my budget and available for four nights. My corner room had two balconies with French doors opening to each. Below, tradesmen, tourists and pilgrims shopped, ate and celebrated the great city, as numerous buskers sang and played their souls into the night. During most of that evening and night I struggled to find the words that I would write in my journal: a chronicle, a record of a journey that had been sixty days of pilgrimage on the Camino de Santiago.

W. Lee Nichols

Day sixty, I wrote; the first of four days to live in Santiago de Compostela, Galicia Spain. Somehow, I am acutely aware that this is not the end of my pilgrimage; it is the beginning. The knowing was deep and fulfilling. It imparted a confidence of oneness and spirit that was both humbling and joyous.

I had brought a small child inside me who was filled with wonder and curiosity; he had been locked in that internal cellar for seventy-two years. Now, he was free to walk in the sunlight of a planet that he loved more than mere words allowed. No language of man could begin to express the multi-dimensions of infinite love that flowed through him for the life and beauty that he now encountered. It was the music of the cosmos and the stars, all in harmony—within one man empowered with bliss.

I surrendered and let the scaffolding of his prison fall away; he stepped free and picked up the discarded body that had imprisoned him and made it his own. For the first time, we now walked as one: whole and integrated, with the passion and curiosity of youth and the wisdom of age, distilled from the long journey in search of enlightenment.

So many simple truths started to become revelations of wisdom and deep inner knowing. The most unexpected, spontaneous emotion was that of humility and a deep reverence of acceptance that extended itself to everything. I am impassioned to document this story of a pilgrimage and the fragile rebirth of a common man, on that speck of stardust, on that infinite journey. To know it, is to share it.

Before starting pilgrimage in Pamplona I had opened the doors to the cellar of my fears and demons. Obviously, I had come to a turning point where I was forced to accept the truth. Life as a cancer-ridden old man, who had lost all his material possessions and social support had little future, if any. All my friends, children and grandchildren were absorbed with successful careers and families of their own. I had become an outsider, alone and afraid of the coming years with no place to call home. It was not intentional that I brought the confessions of failure, fear and fragments of an impersonated life to the camino. I had told myself that this pilgrimage was an affordable last adventure, in a country that I loved, and a language that I understood.

I did not look for, nor did I imagine solutions to my personal problems. I simply opened the doors to the fears, masks and defenses that had held me prisoner with the child inside. The shoddy construction of defensive walls tumbled down. There I stood, naked and exposed, but I promised that I would not build a new mask.

Challenges began immediately, but in the darkest of moments, my pilgrimage provided time to find illuminating solutions. Acceptance of the truth was an obvious hurdle to overcome, and forgiveness became a stumbling stone on my first day out. I reflect that once those two teachers became learned and integrated I began to feel a firm base from which to grow. Suffering became a longer and more difficult challenge since it manifested itself in my body as an experience of pain. It was an enlightened moment when I realized that suffering truly was optional.

Soon, my pilgrimage began to take on a life of its own. I learned how to let go and not be in charge. An invisible but palpable force, a flow of knowing, began to silently guide my choices and actions. As my awareness and acceptance became stronger, so did the flow, with obvious positive reinforcements. I turned to my fellow pilgrims less often for companionship as my daily teachers became the abundance and beauty of nature. There were no bad days. They all brought joy, elation and awe. Every butterfly, insect, stone and mist had its own magic, which I had known in childhood but never imagined that it could be reclaimed. Once, when I was sitting in an endless field of heather on a mountain top, I suddenly burst into tears of joy with an emotional release that I had never known. Not only did the earth accept me, I accepted me and I openly wept in its wisdom. What a simple but powerful and timeless truth it was.

I chose to call my new magic carpet *flow* because that's how smooth and rhythmic it became. I could feel its guidance and energy as a state of wellbeing, euphoria, happiness and most of all, how it connected me to all life and the moment. With flow, every aspect of nature and life filled me with a childlike wonder and awe. When I returned to the United States, I was excited to learn that many others had also discovered flow. Some had lectured and authored well-researched books on the subject.

In *The Power of Flow, Practical Ways to Transform Your Life with Meaningful Coincidence,* the authors, Charlene Belitz and Meg Lundstrom, have interviewed hundreds of people empowered with flow. Their research reveals that nine attributes combine to elevate and maintain flow as a new constant state of being. They have concluded that commitment; honesty, courage, passion, immediacy, openness, receptivity, positivity and trust are the conditions that can awaken us to the natural stream of flow. After reading the *Power of Flow,* I was happy to have words to confirm the force that had empowered my journey. It enabled me to participate in an authentic mindful life with discernment for what really matters.

In Professor Mihaly Csikszentmihalyi's book, *Flow, the Psychology of Optimal Experience,* we learn that flow activities are fun and pleasurable; they lead us to feel euphoric and immensely happy. Play, art, pageantry, ritual and games transport us into a magical zone where we become hyper focused on a specific activity.

He has studied athletes involved in extreme sports such as rock climbing, dare-devil stunts and Olympic-level events where the participants achieved a "zone" or "peak experience." They had been propelled into a new realm of being and energy reserve. Artists, chess players and musicians have all experienced the capacity to enter the same zone of flow where time and physical needs are forgotten. Most of us have experienced a group of jazz musicians as they "zone out" and enter a world of synchronized harmony and intuitive language that defies interpretation. Many times, we the audience, are carried along in the same power of timeless flow. The same thing happens to an audience at major sports events where the energy of flow is so intense in the players that they carry the crowd with them.

Professor Csikszentmihalyi's extensive research has produced several research papers and three bestselling books on flow. His studies reveal that all forms of activity that produced flow resulted in transporting the person into a new reality; an altered state of being that elevated the participant to higher levels of performance. Now, I began to understand the euphoric states of consciousness that I had been experiencing while walking the Camino. Flow is such a powerful energy that it transforms the self into a more complex and synergistic state of awareness. Once we learn to use and maintain a state of flow I believe that we can enter a universal stream of flow activity. Perhaps the sensitivity to communicate with all life and beings can be achieved through the gateway of flow—even talking with cats. In fact, you are reading this book because I lived it in flow, I wrote it in flow, and I let the power of flow publish it. The same force put it in your hands. I never once imagined another outcome.

The unmistaken and obvious synchronicity of flow began to teach this eager pupil not to fear or anticipate. When I allowed concerns for imagined obstacles to become part of decision making, flow either slowed or stopped all together. What I had to learn was to let go, and that always required courage, until trust became a constant friend and reinforcement. During the final few days before arriving in Santiago, my fellow pilgrims spent a lot of time securing confirmed reservations for the next day. Their concern and defined limitations and hardships were always there challenging me to join them, "to be sensible and not get stuck in the open without tent or supplies." I began to see how difficult it would be to change our personal paradigm and accept flow if all who surround us reinforce and mirror their own fears and limitations. For that reason, the camino or similar locations are perfect opportunities to renew and enter a state of flow without the disruption of dogmatic routine and negative feedback.

If I became anxious about a place to stay, the time of day or the actions of others, flow stopped. Soon, I learned to center, let go, and be accepting and not condemning of myself when thoughts went astray. After all, I was human and those feelings were okay. A quick meditation always returned me to a calm state where awareness and flow would be waiting. Walking as a pilgrim for sixty days had nurtured and awakened my child of wonder into the wisdom of adulthood.

At this point, I feel like I have won the lottery. Whatever time that remains for me, even one day, will be greater and more magical than all the years of the past. I have tapped into a resource that continues to teach and guide my journey. Its vibration and harmony create patterns of flow and resistances inherent to all beings, all space, all time. I have been riding a wave of continuous synchronistic patterns that are unmistakably beyond chance. Chance is fifty-fifty; it feels as though I have been surfing on a crest of one hundred. In four days I will continue this journey, on an uncharted odyssey, which will allow the guidance of flow to direct and reveal the lessons that I am to learn. Being on a true pilgrimage has taught me the courage and awareness to accept an adventure without question or expectations.

Part Three
The Odyssey

"The road goes ever on and on
Down from the door where it began,
Now far ahead the road has gone,
And I must follow, if I can,
Pursuing it with wary feet,
Until it joins some larger way,
Where many paths and errands meet,
And whither then? I cannot say.
J. R. R. Tolkein ~ the Lord of the Rings

23

SANTIAGO DE COMPOSTELA

*Ordinary men hate solitude. But the Master
makes use of it, embracing his aloneness,
realizing he is one with the Universe.*
~Lao Tzu

Angela and Rafa, from Barcelona, invited me to lunch at a favorite café where they had dined during previous trips to Santiago. The Gato Negro is also a favorite for locals, where fresh seafood is prepared in the traditional Galician style of cookery. We slurped down two platters of miniature clams, a platter of steamed mussels and a plate of pimentos Pardon before tackling variations of the Galician stuffed pie known as empanadas. In the Americas, an empanada is a small pastry filled with either a sweet or savory. The Galician version is most often filled with seafood, with meat being a distant second choice. It is baked on a large sheet pan or pizza pan, and served in slices. We sampled three classic versions, stuffed with sweet red peppers and onions, as well as a choice of octopus, sardines or tuna. Another specialty of the house was local chorizo sausage simmered in red wine; the dark red reduction infused with garlic. Two pitchers of house wine from the barrel and a platter of cheese with membrillo quince jelly completed a feast to remember.

Reluctant to say farewell, we took brandy and coffee in luxury at a Viennese style coffee house, The Café Casino. We lounged late in the afternoon discussing our journeys on the camino. They had taken the primitive route down from the north coast through the Principality of Asturias. As Rafa finished describing their adventures and sharing photos, I was excited and ready to leave and follow their path. As we prepared to leave with hugs and plans to be in touch, Rafa said, "I think that you would really enjoy Oviedo. For some reason I am inspired to say that it's the place you're looking for." Angela gave a knowing nod in agreement. "It's one of our favorite cities. Something is very special there. You have to experience it to understand," she said.

The city suffers few quiet moments. Pilgrims arrive daily during all hours, anxious and excited to be in the sacred holy city; they come here first, eat, party and wander the city gaping in awe at its great cathedral and medieval streets. They have forgotten that their backpacks still cling to their shoulders and they have no place to rest. Weeks of walking, suffering, and sacrifice have delivered them to this fabled city of Saint James. Every great journey has tales to tell and nothing can stop them when old friends are discovered on the narrow cobblestone streets of a faraway land. The excitement of celebration and laughter below my balcony became a soundtrack of pleasant background fugues as they drifted up and entwined into my own dream fantasies.

For four days, I walked and explored the old town of Santiago. The cathedral alone required three visits to tour the Portico de la Gloria, the museum, treasury, crypt and Santiago's tomb where his relics repose in a silver casket. The more intimate Plaza das Praterias flanks one side of the cathedral, where it hosts a continuous flow of concerts, vaudeville and, on one occasion, a juried antique car show with drivers in period costume. The plaza is dominated with a twenty-foot sculpted stone fountain featuring life size horses spewing water into its great basin.

The city is enriched with several great museums. The park of Santo Domingo de Bonaval houses two of my favorites. The Modern Contemporary Museum features current and cutting-edge Spanish explorations into twenty-first century art and its relationship to global expressions of modernism. The fine ethnic museum, just across the street, is housed in a handsome renovated section of the antique Convent of Santo Domingo. It is one of the best and most informative ethnic museums anywhere. Here, you can see a well-documented history of the Galician Celts. I left with a greater understanding and appreciation for some of the curious buildings and customs that I had encountered while passing through Galicia's remote mountain villages. The rich cultural diversity of the Spanish Celts was so very similar to my own heritage distilled in Appalachia from Irish-English ancestors.

There was an eclectic mix of color and vibrancy in the daily experience of just being in Santiago, it would fill volumes of memories. I allowed each day to provide its many rewards of discovery as I wandered the streets and plazas. Santiago has the ability to stage events that appear to be very spontaneous; professional and extremely cinematic at the same time. For example, the car show was staged with a red, carpeted entrance and a host wearing white tie and tails. The great fountain, cathedral and wide steps became the show's stage and props—everything appearing to be at perfect camera angles of sight and lighting. Two hours before I had walked through the same plaza, where there was no indication that such an event was about to happen.

Another time, on a walk to the bookstore I turned a corner to encounter a full orchestra set up in the street. There was no plaza, just a wide street with medieval arcades on both sides filled with busy shops and cafés. Folks who lived upstairs in the buildings brought out chairs, sipped on wine and stopped everything to enjoy the music and become a community where time stopped. "What century is this?" I thought.

That evening, I sat at a street café with a new tablet to journal the continuous flow of observations that filled my mind and memory. I was just beginning to identify the source of my happiness and wonder since the grace of flow had started directing my journey. My attention was drawn to a lone bagpiper who stood under the arch of the stone arcade. He was backlit in the soft glow of the nearby street lantern, an upturned hat on the cobblestones at his feet and he played from the heart to an audience that didn't have time to stop and listen. *Amazing Grace* had never been more profound or welcome.

Without instructions or a map of willful intention, I had created the conditions for happiness in my life. In reflection, that equates to baking your first cake without a recipe. What are the odds of getting it right without experimentation? Surely the many ingredients that I used had to be assembled in the correct order and given enough time to bake. The amazing grace of my journey flowed with thoughts of wondering how I could share this journey and leave a map, a recipe for others to follow and find their bliss. The flow of one man's happiness can become a river when shared with truth and compassion. As the Buddha has taught, "All that we are is a result of what we have thought." Tonight I was filled with humble thoughts of gratitude for the gift of awareness, of being. I was savoring a slice of a timeless cosmic cake, one that continues to replenish itself for eternity. Even more importantly; there is enough for everyone to join the feast and remain at the table.

The craggy headlands know as Finisterre, on the westernmost shores of Spain's Galician coast, holds many myths and legends of pagan ritual and early hermits. In pre-Christian Roman times it was a major port and village. But the Celts and their Druid priests were there long before that. Great sacred stones and altars, where their sacrifices called to the setting sun and prayed for its return remain on the hilltops. Since antiquity, pilgrims have continued their walk from Santiago to pray, cleanse and watch the sun go home into the darkness of an unknown mythical void. Most people walk the hilly fifty miles in three days but that's a stretch for those who want to explore or have problems with intermittent steep and rocky terrain. Armed with my new toolbox of awareness and the power of flow, I left on a clear Monday morning. Where better to continue my journey than at "The End of the World?"

24

FINISTERRE, THE END OF THE (KNOWN) WORLD

Go find yourself first so you can also find me.
~Rumi

The call to adventure was strong but I didn't feel comfortable or at home on this new section of the camino leading to Finisterre. I was happy; in fact, I was joyous to return to walking and the path of discovery that two months on pilgrimage had instilled. However, some inner voice acted like a personal compass trying to nudge me back on a more direct path. The shaded, woodland road was pleasant and filled with songbirds and small streams. What could be missing?

Several fellow pilgrims were walking with a lighter step than before, as though this was their morning stroll. Gone was the rush, the blisters and the pull of Santiago to complete their pilgrimage. Now they were tourists on a stroll through the woods, where visions of camaraderie and good times lay on the near horizon. They were in happy moods with conversations about sundrenched sandy beaches and a few beers.

The most common question after greeting was, "Where are you going to stay?"

I had not even considered making a reservation; flow had provided for me on the pilgrimage, and I assumed it would continue. That said, it was mid-summer and Finesterre did have a reputation for overflowing with the combination of tourists and pilgrims. The popularity of the seaside resort had forced the local hostel to allow only those who had walked from Santiago; and had had their new Finesterre passport stamped at all locations along the way.

For some reason still unknown but to the flow that guided me, I had a strong urge to leave the path and take a bus out of the next village. I didn't need to prove that I could walk to the end of the world. I knew I could. "Good luck, they might let you sleep on the beach," one of my companions on the path called out when I boarded the bus headed to Finisterre.

The bus soon came to the bay where it followed the convolutions of the many coves and inlets that connected the small villages fronting the Atlantic coastline. So did the camino. We passed dozens of pilgrims where the only path was on the highway. Finisterre sits on the final, fish-shaped piece of the headland where the village hugs the narrow tail section in its southern cove. It is just a quarter mile walk through town to reach the white sands of Praia do Mar de Fora on the opposite shores of the Atlantic. The finger of land rises on high rocky cliffs and continues three more miles west into the sun. With dramatic visual displays of high cliffs on both sides, it summits at Mount Facho, and like a great whale, plunges into the sea at the faro (lighthouse) at Cabo Finesterre.

The bus pulled into town and reversed itself to back down a street that ended at the wharf. It was shocking to see so many people in so few clothes. The crowds spilled out of cafés, bars and hostels into the sun-drenched street and onto the wharf, like little children playing in a sandbox. I let the anxious young passengers get off first and then stepped to the side of the bus to retrieve my backpack.

A dignified, middle-aged woman approached and watched as I shouldered my bag.

"Sir, do you have a reserved room?" she asked.

Talking With Cats

"No ma'am, I will be looking for one," I told her.

"I have three rooms with bath in my home that I rent. One just became available. In fact, the young man who had it is just now boarding this bus. They have their own private kitchen and living area," she continued. She wanted me to see the location and inspect the room before further discussion. So, like old friends we left together, walking up the street discussing village life.

I had learned not to question the miraculous results of flow, but I couldn't help feeling excited as my trust and acceptance once again received its reward. The three-storied modern home was a short distance up the hill, overlooking the town and the waterfront. It was fenced with a large security gate. The accommodations were so luxurious that I had a flash of concern that it would be over my meager budget.

"We charge very little because my husband is an attorney who needs the tax benefits of a rental property. I have two maids so there is no extra work for me. Would fifteen Euros a night be acceptable?" she asked, as though reading my thoughts.

The remaining two rooms were occupied with a senior couple from Canada and a teacher from Germany. The Canadians had been on the camino for many weeks, having trekked from France, through Santiago and on to Finesterre. The fortyish teacher had walked the Portuguese Camino north to Santiago and bused to Finesterre. He had ended a twenty-year relationship, which had left him feeling empty and at a major crossroad in his life. Here, even more than in Santiago, he sought atonement and direction for an uncertain future. The well-equipped kitchen provided a common ground for friendship as we prepared and shared local cheese, wine and stories from the road.

If Santiago conferred a bachelor's degree for pilgrimage, then Finesterre gives a masters class in spiritual energy and the plurality of the universe. The two unique locations are complimentary and deeply connected as they prepare and instruct all willing seekers. Having followed the progressive journey in the traditional fashion, I cannot imagine one without the other. The camino calms the mind, strengthens the body and brings its pilgrims home to a humble grace and acceptance of being. Historically, metaphorically and spiritually, Finesterre has been a location for contemplating the unknown and the magical worlds of both light and darkness. Here we can challenge our angels and demons alike—and sip wine with both.

It's a three-mile-walk up Mount Facho where the remainder of the headland rises on high, vertical rocky cliffs to point directly into the setting sun. At the very tip, sitting on cliffs several hundred feet above the raging Atlantic waves, is the faro or lighthouse.

Below, perhaps one hundred feet down the rocks, a crude pit smoldered with clothing items and notes to the gods from pilgrims who had cleansed themselves of personal past. This was not new. Historical records and archeological evidence confirm that from time immemorial, worshipers have come to this spot to watch the great golden sun descend into darkness at the end of the world. They built ceremonial fires of cleansing and initiation to seek guidance and empowerment for their own journeys. After all, the sun-god needed to be invited back to continue his daily blessings of warmth, life and light. It is in such a place as this, where the universal duality of sacred opposites meet to become a synergistic force, that man has historically come to feed his soul. It is a location where the known and the un-known have shared the same feast. Here amongst the sacred stones of Mount Facho was the oracle at the End of the World.

The sheer cliffs are steep but have many ledges and caves along the way down to the blue-green waves that pound away at their base. There is no path, but some pilgrims will try to find footings to climb down as far as possible. I discovered some of the vegetation had strong, deep roots to prevent slipping as I maneuvered in a zigzag descent around the ledges. Each time I came to the end, another possibility down to the next ledge became evident. Eventually, I was completely alone, having passed the last pilgrim sitting on a ledge playing his guitar and singing to the goddess of westerly wind. I found a deep, recessed outcropping that was sheltered from the gales. It also had a shelf suspended out and above the sea and rocks that gave me a panoramic view of infinite wave-tossed ocean and the retreating headlands to the east.

During meditation, a sense of presence came over me. I could feel a new energy, but could hear or see no physical confirmation. I remained seated, but with eyes open and soon fell under the spell of the seagulls as they floated up past my ledge, only to hover completely still, midflight as their cocked heads eyed the various outcroppings. Once again, I became aware of some movement; this time on a ledge to my right. When I looked, nothing was there and how could there be anything there? This ledge was a thin shelf that gave me vertigo just to look at it. A few large boulders to the backside and an overhang suggested that the ledge might be the aerie porch to a cave.

Again, movement came to the ledge, something large and white, but definitely not human—just to disappear within the boulders before I could identify any anatomical parts. The mystery beast had my undivided, unblinking attention. I was soon rewarded with a full view of a great horned goat as he walked to the front and laid down with his front legs crossed and dangling over the edge, like a cat. "So this is my totem for today," I thought. The epitome of courage and trust, at one in the universe: he was proud and regal, but wise and modest in the acceptance of his throne. I saw him with a new appreciation and awareness, that we are all gods, at one with all beings and all knowing.

The summit of Mount Facho has twin peaks spaced like eyes on an alligator, with a small valley etched between them. On the south peak is the fifth century remains of Ermita de San Guillerme (Hermitage of Saint William) and the north peak still wears the crown of sacred stones, worshiped by pagan Romans, Phoenicians and Druids—and home to a fabled witch. I packed a lunch of meats, cheese, bread, fruit and wine and hiked the mountain to spend the day and evening as an initiate to their wisdom. At the top I was able to walk to one of the earliest Christian sites and one of the earliest pagan sites of worship in Europe. The fact that there were artifacts from both cultures to see, touch and explore made the trip even more sensory and rewarding.

Pilgrims streamed up the lower road to the lighthouse and the cape's cliffs, but none climbed the peaks to explore two of the most important sacred power-points on earth. Left alone, I was on an adventure to take communion with the spirits of light and shadow, of earth and transcendence.

The bare, windswept ruin of the Hermitage of Saint William was somewhat sheltered, having been built on the leeward side of a great boulder. The lonely hilltop was sacred even then. It could also have been chosen as a place of renewal, allowing the old hermit to face the rebirth of each day's sunrise.

The mythology of the region has Saint James preaching at this spot and at a village nearby where ancient seafarers stopped for fresh water, supplies and rest. This had been a sacred place of worship and would certainly have been well-known to him. Many Christians believe that James was only following in the footsteps of his master, who is believed to have studied with the Druid priests of Galicia and at Cornwall in the Isles of Britannia. Opportunities for Jesus to have traveled this way during his eighteen-years of pilgrimage were well established and possible.

Nearby rests a powerful statement of both pagan and Christian ritual, embraced together in a fertility rite. The stone plinth, known as Saint William's bed, has for centuries drawn couples who were infertile to copulate and conceive on its surface. Locals claim that barren lovers still come here to conceive and receive the powers of "love on the rocks."

I sat between the great boulder and the large pile of stones that once was a hermitage. "Come, join me Saint William. I have fine spirits of good wine to share with you." I announced, and spilled some on one of the stones for his pleasure. It was good to enjoy a fine lunch with an old friend.

At the highest point of Mount Facho, the cliffs drop straight away to the sea below. Sitting on the rim are three groups of rocks that are the size of elephants and many tons in weight. They are stacked and arranged in families as though the gods had placed them there. Some are in the shape of twenty foot-anvils and sit piggy-back on yet greater stones. Others are natural viewing stones where the sun records the seasons in its annual arc across the heavens. No wonder so many cultures considered them sacred. Not only was the sun a god, here they could watch him go to bed in what literally was then the very edge of the earth. The natural combination of elements is so awe-inspiring that surely this is the place to become whole with one's god.

Since prehistoric times, humans have made pilgrimage to the very power spot where I stood. They came as I did, to seek understanding, wisdom and enlightenment at the altar of mysteries and pray to gods greater than they could imagine. The rocks and cliffs at Cabo Finesterre became one of the holiest and most venerated places on earth during the Middle Ages.

For me, it had lost none of its power or magic. The winds sang divine music as they wound their way east through the rock formations, and the tides thundered sonorous bass notes as they climbed the cliffs below. How could I refuse to join the symphony of life and freedom that held me so closely in its embrace?

According to legends and recorded tales from knights and monks of the middle ages, there lived a very nasty witch nearby. Orcavella's home was a cave on the cliffs, just a few yards west of the Sacred Stones. (It is now fenced within the grounds of a communications tower.) The legend goes that once she grew old and tired of raiding the villages for children to eat, the cave became her stone tomb where she remained among the undead. Thereafter, she lured hapless men into her enticing embraces so she could smother them in the crypt of morbid love. It was reported that shepherds who heard the calls for help, only found a sepulcher with a great stone over its entrance surrounded with many serpents and vipers.

On my last day in Finisterre, Sebastian, my teacher friend from Germany, and I shared a long breakfast. Our conversations in philosophy and religion challenged both of us as we searched for the correct words in English to describe our feelings and pilgrimage. The Galician gift of fog, rain and mist held the village in a dense cloud, eliminating external plans and activities.

"If the weather clears, I would like to invite you to join me in a farewell ceremony on the beach at sunset," he proposed.

"That'll be a perfect farewell and I'm honored to accept. Let's imagine the most perfect sunset, which will be so magical we are unable to anticipate its glory," I announced in a teasing voice.

He laughed at all my English superlatives and reminded me, "Keep the words simple and kindergarten like. I don't teach English, you know."

By late morning the rain had stopped and the clouds lifted from the valley floor, but the mist and fog remained. I left to explore the fishing village and tidelands to the east. When I arrived at the docks, a perfect circle of blue sky opened directly over the bay and let a shaft of sunlight slide through to illuminate the little flotilla at the marina. Many of the small brightly-painted boats had returned to the large warehouse on the dock, where the fishermen's collective iced and received their daily catch.

At that moment and still today in my memory, Finisterre is one of the most beautiful little fishing villages in the world. There are no high-rise buildings and no modern services to encourage heavy tourism, which would disrupt the tranquility. So there it sits: a sleepy little village, with colorful boats in its harbor, sheltered in the embrace of a sacred mountain at the end of the world. I was bewitched.

I left the wharf and headed through neighborhoods and homes and shops that clung to the waterfront going east near the highway that had brought me in. Soon, I had to either go through the tidal basin for two miles or walk beside the highway. My child came alive, as I jumped between pools on algae-covered rocks and splashed in the cool water. An aquarium of sea life had been left in the basins after high-tide and I took time to agitate and become acquainted with every one of them that didn't hide. "Wake up, I want to get to know you," I told them. Sometimes the sea would rush through a rock formation and show-off with a little geyser for a finale. Even the gurgling and splashing became special sounds, the language of mother earth as she told her own story of pilgrimage.

My wandering eventually led to Praia de Langosteira, the favored and safer beach for swimming. It was bordered with an ellipse of white sand, and wore a collar of pastel seashells, freshly deposited by the tides. To my surprise, no pilgrims or tourists were there. Just a few Spanish families with children swam and played near the rock formations that bordered the tidal pools. As I returned to the town center, I checked bus schedules. Murcia (or Muxia in Galician), a village thirty miles to the north, had a strong magnetic pull on my senses and imagination. I would follow my journey there tomorrow.

Sunset had been occurring at five minutes past ten. Blue skies were still opening across the western horizon as Sebastian and I left the house at nine-fifteen through the weed path to the rear of the house. As we crossed the narrow piece of headland behind the village, our trail opened to a wider one of gravel and stone. At the sand cliffs overlooking the sea, we entered a well-constructed, elevated boardwalk that prevented people from damaging or disturbing the delicate dunes and grasses that held them in place.

The Praia do Mar de Fora is a natural wonder. It is wide and deep, in the shape of a smile, with large handsome rock formations in the corners of its mouth. The fluffy, white sand beach continues back to the dunes and cliffs where a few celebrants had built a fire at the mouth of one of the sea caves. The pancake-shaped waves flowed across the sand in shallow and mysterious patterns that continued for at least two hundred feet. Further out, the water was dangerous, with deadly undertows. Warnings had been posted around the village. Because of this and the hundreds of shipwrecks that lay at the bottom of the deceptive tranquil scene, its Spanish name is the Coast of Death.

I left Sebastian alone with his personal farewell ceremony of wine and meditation. I sensed that his loss, ability to forgive and fears of a questionable future were coming to a head. He needed the time and courage to confront them without interruption. We agreed to find each other later.

I trekked through the packed, wet sand to the rock formations that extended from the tall cliffs and disappeared into the sea at the western-most corner of the beach's mouth. I sat in meditation on a great rock where emerald waves splashed seaweed around its base. The sun shimmered: a bright orange orb, hovering just above the horizon line for a timeless moment before it started to disappear. The entire beach became golden and the mist that hovered above the water suddenly became a veil of shimmering droplets in the fading light. A lone, three-year-old girl ran and played in the distant shallow waves as though life and energy would never end. Perhaps, she had the answer all along.

Sebastian was sitting alone in a nest of dry sand. He was precisely half way-down the beach and half-way between the sea and the cliffs. No one remained except the small tribe with the bonfire at the cliff's edge. Without words, I joined my friend. We both had taken an immense journey of soul-searching and reflection during the past few hours. Now we were content to sit in the warm sand and watch the long and varied wave patterns at sea. As darkness settled in the horizon turned to a blue glow that was captured and repeated in the hovering mist. As one: we both became aware of a new light, coming from behind us—falling across our shoulders and casting faint shadows across the sand.

The goddess gave us her blessings as a full moon rose behind us on the eastern horizon. Her majestic luminosity seemed to fill the clear sky, with the exception of an escort of small clouds on both sides—their angelic shapes fringed in the golden light. I knew, and Sebastian knew that we were not alone. We walked back that night united in the same wisdom, wonder and state of being that the Druid priests, the hermits, the Christians and the pagans had all come for. For all of us, life on earth is the gift. When we awaken to its flow and guidance, we become enlightened beings—humbled and filled with the gratitude of awareness.

25

MURCIA (MUXIA), SYNCHRONICITY AND FLOW

When we love, we always strive to become better than we are. When we strive to become better than we are, everything around us becomes better too.
~Paulo Coelho, the Alchemist

The bus wound its way north along farm tracks and through forests before arriving in the village of Muxia. Like Finisterre, the town sits on rocky cliffs at the tip of another headland, not as westerly but also dramatically beautiful. Here, no kind woman came to welcome my arrival and escort me to her home. I shouldered the backpack and set out to allow my intuitive inner voice to direct and locate the energy and flow that I knew would be waiting to guide me.

Half-way down a commercial street lined with cafés and shops, the voice said, "Turn around and go back." I followed my intuition. At the next street I turned left, went up the hill, made a right turn and headed in the direction of the Sanctuario at the overlook. I instinctively followed it as though I were on the way home. Within two blocks, a new building stood out as strangely familiar. The feeling was so profound that it made me stop and ask the question, "Have I been here before?" A simple, black-lettered sign announced my arrival at the Xunta Bela Muxia, and Beautiful Murcia it was.

I didn't know if this location held a clue as to where I was to go, or if, in fact, I had arrived. The Camino had taught me not to anticipate and to always frame my thoughts, statements and questions as possibilities.

I walked into the modern albergue and told them the truth. "I didn't walk here, so I'm not qualified to stay as a pilgrim; perhaps you could direct me to a public hostel or pension?"

The congenial host rose from his desk and came around to shake my hand. "Sir, this is where you should stay. We are not full. Come let me show you our facilities."

The dorm had two double bunk beds for each open cubicle, except for the one closest to the windows. That section held a single double bunk bed with a commanding view over the village. Furthermore, both the upper and lower bunks were available. I immediately became attracted to the space and the bottom bunk. In silent recognition of my thoughts, the host invited me to make it my home.

I laid my gear on the bed and left for the rest room. When I returned, there was an object lying on the window sill in front of the bunk I had chosen. It was a smooth, kidney-shaped stone with a blood red stain naturally infused within the central section. I picked up the talisman gently, as though it were fragile or a small bird. It fell across my palm in a natural, almost organic fusion, when my fingers closed and held it tightly. It had a force and energy as though it were alive; maybe a spirit or baby dragon slumbered inside.

This must be what the ring of power feels like, I thought. Neither the host, housekeeper, nor nearby occupants had ever seen the stone. The housekeeper declared that she had wiped that very sill just a few hours before and she was certain nothing was there then. My host smiled. "Well, I guess the stone is meant for you," he said and returned to receiving new guests.

Muxia is a quintessential Galician fishing village and has not been exploited and overrun with commercial greed or flashy tourist accommodations. The village straddles a central spine that runs the length of the narrow headland, giving the town two waterfronts, one on the south-west side and one on the north-east.

The stony spine comes to a dramatic and spectacular crescendo at the western tip where the rocky outcroppings become accessible flat shelves, thrust out into the frothy aquamarine waves of the Atlantic. Standing atop the terraced flat stones, giant house-size boulders lay scattered in formations that catch the incoming waves at angles that maximize their force. The drama provides a constant symphony of energy in high flying froth and foam. Because of its cinematic and accessible beauty this was the stand-in for Finisterre in the dramatic ending of the movie, *The Way*.

The Santiago pilgrimage is uniquely entwined within the myths of Saint James and his connection to Muxia. The name itself is a derivation of the Galician word *Mongia*, land of monks, an imprint left from a nearby twelfth century monastery. Saint James is said to have come to Muxia, discouraged and disappointed, to renew his faith and to rest and recover from exhaustive preaching among the pagans. While praying at the shore for guidance, a vision of the Virgin Mary appeared, coming toward him in a boat from the sea.

The legend of Our Lady of the Boat stands today, a miracle manifest in a shipwreck of rocks that are believed to be the Virgin's petrified boat. The tallest triangular stone, with obvious similarities to a ship's sail, is known as the Pedra dos Cadris. The sacred stone sail is said to heal rheumatic ailments when believers pass under the formation nine times. The beautiful eighteenth century Santuario da Virxe da Barca (Sanctuary of the Virgin of the Boat) stands near the tip of the rocky promontory within a few yards of the ocean waves.

I spent several hours that afternoon within the shelter of the giant mega-ton rocks that welcomed the thunderous waves splashing all around me. It was as though I had become fluid also; my mind flowed with long-forgotten information gleaned from a lifetime of reading. I imagined that my brain was reorganizing and prioritizing every experience and teaching during the seventy-two years of my journey. I wanted to write it all down, less the spell would lift and I might awaken from a dream that had forgotten its story.

Before the Camino, I had information. Now that I had had several weeks alone to deconstruct and eliminate the clutter and constant chatter of my mind, I had clarity of thought. In the absence of anxiety and fear, my days flowed with distilled, functional guidance. Information that I once knew as mere common knowledge became filtered into observations, acceptance and awareness. No longer encumbered with possessions or distractions, I had found happiness and joy in everything that I encountered. Finally, I understood and assimilated the teachings of Jesus and Buddha. I recall a statement made by the Buddhist master, Thich Nhat Hanh, "Many people are alive but they don't touch the miracle of being alive." Another of his teachings now rang true for me, "Enlightenment is always there. Small enlightenment will bring great enlightenment. If you breathe in and are aware that you are alive—then you can touch the miracle of being alive—then that is a kind of enlightenment."

The truth that awakened, guided and comforted me was no longer 'I'. Somewhere I had surrendered the ego and released the energy of 'I' to become a mere unit of being, within an infinite universe of being. My identity was at one, the same as the waves, rocks and all that my eyes and imagination could survey. The conscious download of becoming, confirmed every being I encountered as me, and I as them. Sometimes I felt bewildered, like a child in kindergarten, but I was clothed in joy and happiness with what I was learning.

When I returned to the albergue, the reason I had been guided to Bela Muxia became apparent. Kimberly, from San Francisco, and Pamela, from France, had arrived and occupied the two bunks that were stacked against our shared dividing wall. They had just met for the first time but had fallen into immediate déjà vu recognition of each other that included me when I walked in. Neither of us pretended to understand the magical spell that our little threesome came under. We didn't need to; our friendship and acceptance did not require a reason for being. Intuitively, we responded to each other with an overflow of wisdom, shared journey and spiritual insights that became empowered in a synergistic group oneness. Carl Jung wrote about similar meetings,

"Synchronicity is the coming together of inner and outer events in a way that cannot be explained by cause and effect and that is meaningful to the observer."

We formed a triangle of three archetypes: Pamela was a middle-aged earth goddess, whose nurturing and timeless wisdom flowed from magic potions of kindness and compassion. Her sincere spiritual energy and warm smile embraced all who entered its shelter. Kimberly was the practical youth, the scholar who asked wise questions, she embodied the wisdom of becoming, in search of a dependable structure to support it. She had robed herself with a mantle of courage and joy, and she knew that her pilgrimage did not end in Santiago. I, as the third leg of that cosmic milk stool, brought an old Shaman's bag of oracle bones, to serve as an interpretive connection between earth, knowledge and spiritual becoming.

The three of us walked to the sea that evening. We sat on top of the great rocks at sunset, watching the shimmering sun god drop into the sea, and we waited in its afterglow as darkness crept across the waves. We were there to welcome the moon-goddess as she rose behind us. She came full and radiant, her great energy pulling at the tides as though they were but a bucket-full of spring water. There, in that little fishing village, the stars dazzled and danced around a full moon that filled more of the heavenly space than any of us had ever seen before. Awed by the wonder of being in the presence of nature's majesty, we spoke little about what we understood and knew to be true within each other's hearts. It was enough, after all the centuries as timeless wave forms, to once again sit together at the edge of a great sea, silently recalling our collective journeys as star travelers.

We walked back to the village along the seawall as the moon skipped shards of twinkling beams across the rippled waters of the bay. When we approached the settlement, ethereal music from a choir in rehearsal floated down to the street from the open windows of a seaside building. Captured under the spell of moonlight with an angelic soundtrack, we stood transfixed under the open windows and applauded with joyous enthusiasm. I went to sleep reflecting on the mysteries and wonder of a universe that would gather the souls of three humble humans and awaken them to each other again. This class is not over, I thought.

There will be other times, other places, other dreams to work together on. We are but three of many.

In eighteen hours from when we met, we gathered for breakfast to say goodbye to Kimberly. She would bus to Finisterre for a few days before departing to Santiago and a flight home. It was unexpected but completely natural for me to say, "Goodbye daughter, journey well and know I love you."

Pamela and I walked back to the headlands where we climbed the goliath rocks and played in the small basins of captured tidal waters. We hid amongst the great boulders as they sent waves and spray thirty feet into the air all around us. The reason for being there was to return to the waters of life and celebrate our reunion in a christening of bare feet, hands and heart. Hours passed as we savored the short time together; we let go of linear time, letting everything unfold in the moment. We had entered a magical space, as though it were seen through a camera, with Vaseline smeared on its lens. Our parting required no assurances of future meetings. We both knew that our lives unfolded outside of time, where spirits converge as one.

For me, this journey began with loss and surrender. Now it seems as though my whole life has prepared me for it. Perhaps it has. The deep longing and search conducted by my soul has come home to find its answer within. Its message of being truly alive has been the simplest and greatest gift that anyone can receive and it comes wrapped in the fancy paper and ribbons of sustainable joy and happiness.

This pilgrimage has taught me that to remain in flow requires what Buddha, the prophets and sages have always told us; think and remain in a positive state of the moment, the now. Flow empowers us when we align ourselves with visions, positive thoughts, dreams of happiness, joy and the natural world. The more we remain in that state, the greater our love and compassion for all beings. In one way or another we are all connected, transcendent creatures that are capable of great creativity in our short lifespans. I have simply learned to surrender to its mystery.

The journey has made clear that the truth we discover is our truth, the joy we discover is our joy, and that we are worthy of living an authentic life filled with happiness. When we follow our bliss, the quest takes us on a mythical journey where we discover that the magic has always been within us. We can't study for it, or take a class to awaken and become enlightened to our inner wisdom. We must take the journey and quest with the sincerity to accept the truth that peers back from our mirror. The mythologist, Joseph Campbell concluded, "We're not on our journey to save the world but to save ourselves, but in doing that you save the world. The influence of a vital person vitalizes."

My journey has just begun.

A Note to the Reader

Thank You

Words are powerful tools that can change lives, build nations and bring people together in ways we could never have imagined just a few decades ago. Although we may well be a global virtual community of millions of people, we still reach out and touch each other with videos, social pages, blogs and books that open our gifts and hearts to each other and the world.

Thank you for reading my book, a simple story about a common old man who has found healing and happiness through the act of walking, meditating and being mindful of the wonder and magic life on earth has to offer. I invite you to share the joy of my journey by taking time to have one of your own. In the meantime, your kind words in the form of a review on your social network, bookseller's web site or blog will be sincerely appreciated. The wind that lifts my wings continues to be the good deeds, wishes and thoughts of others. We are still a tribe, grateful for each other and the journeys we can share.

Your letters and comments are welcome.

W. Lee Nichols
Post Office Box 1404 Flat Rock NC 28731
Visit our reviews and blog at www.enchantedjourney.org

Gratitudes & Acknowledgements

This journal of pilgrimage and awakening on the Camino de Santiago started writing itself at 33,000 feet in the air on my way home from Spain. It would not stop. Day and night, for five months, I was thrilled and happy to relive and retrace my journey as I transcribed my journals to manuscript.

It did not happen alone or without a superb support team: First and foremost, I want to thank my fine proofreaders and dear friends; Niki Nichols and Gail Xandy. Thank you to friend and Editor Sally Hudson for transforming my words into a meaningful flow of thought and coherent grammar. Sincere thanks to Bob and Maggie Ferreira, for your unwavering friendship and guidance through it all. Thank you to the professional staff and design team at Balboa Press and Hay House. Every new author should be so lucky to work with you.

Support and love from my wonderful children and grandchildren were the true inspirations to take my pilgrimage in the first place. I could not imagine leaving them with an unfinished epitaph, a life without promise or hope. My dreams were still inside, unopened and unexamined. I love you. Thanks to Giovanni and Tina Nichols Murillo for holding my hand through the darkest of hours. You made me laugh and gave me courage. My eternal gratitude and love to Anthony, Susan and Harper Nichols for your support, love and company, especially through my surgery and recovery. My love to Christopher and Nicole Bryant with every wish for magic and wonder as you begin brave new journeys. Theresa Murillo, I walked this path for you.

Thank you, Niki, for fifty years of friendship, wisdom and the enrichment of our unique and wonderful genetic recipe. The seeds of our legacy and dreams will continue building the bridges of change and hope for a courageous and vital new world. We have always believed and trusted that the hillsides and meadows of wildflowers would bloom again.

Thanks to Sarah Williams, Sandy and Lee Webster and Cynthia Adler for your love, encouragement, shelter and timeless friendship. Special thanks to Brian Hopper for his excellent advice. To Prem Krishnan and Marcos Campos, a big thanks for your friendship, wisdom and patience as I struggled to understand flow and quantum physics. Thank you to Christie and Joel Manners and Robert and Ozlem Mahmood Carlson for including me in your tribe. Last but certainly not least, a thank you beyond words to Lisa Lai and Mark Ye; you not only made my journey possible, your encouragement, friendship and love gave life to my dreams.

Thank you to all the volunteers and staff on the Camino de Santiago. Your consistent acts of kindness cannot be equaled elsewhere. To the people of Spain, you are one of the greatest, kindest and most hospitable cultures on earth. I loved your history, food and ability to stop and smell the roses. No one could forget the nun who said "Sir, just relax your aches and pains here. Let us take care of you."

Resources

The popularity of the Camino de Santiago has seen an equal increase of new literature on the subject. Of the many guides and references used to take my pilgrimage and to produce this book, a few stand out as superior tools to fully inform and safely guide any person on their journey.

John Brierley's *A Pilgrim's Guide to the Camino de Santiago* has set the standard as a "take-with-you" indispensable daily reference. It is laid out in an easy to follow thirty-three day journey but is easily adjusted in either direction. Maps, elevation guides, water fountains, what-to-take, and the paths are so well illustrated that most of us on the camino called it our Bible. For those who might walk the additional few miles to Finisterre and Muxia, be sure and take Brierley's *A Pilgrim's Guide to the Camino Finisterre*. It's a small little book that makes the history and pilgrimages to those two towns come alive.

Before taking pilgrimage on The Camino Francés, please read *The Pilgrimage Road to Santiago, the Complete Cultural Handbook* by David M. Gitlitz and Linda Kay Davidson. This is not a book to carry with you but within its 440 pages you will learn more about the history, art, architecture, geology, folklore and the flora and fauna than a Spanish professor knows. The camino will come alive for readers of this well researched book and they will be so smug and grateful to be this well prepared.

Another book to read before departing on any journey, travel, pilgrimage, or just a stroll down a country lane, is *The Art of Pilgrimage, the seekers guide to Making Travel Sacred* by Phil Cousineau. This book is wise. Cousineau, having been on his own journey for a few lifetimes, tells great travel stories and he understands our wanderlust and the hunger of our souls. Most folks don't know how to travel or make pilgrimage. This book will inspire them to learn and enhance their awareness.

Perhaps there is no better way to prepare our mind and heart for walking and pilgrimage than by reading Dr. Wayne Dyer's, *Change Your Thoughts, Change Your Life*. I downloaded the Kindle version on my tablet before departure and found it to be the ultimate mindful guide on a powerful path of awakening to the spirit and wisdom of the Tao.

Most countries have an association to assist pilgrims and travelers with information and support for all the routes of pilgrimage to Santiago de Compostela. For North America, I highly recommend *American Pilgrims on the Camino* (http://www.americanpilgrims.com) they can provide credentials and all the information and support necessary to plan an unforgettable journey. To learn more about the Camino, several local chapters are located throughout the United States. Their meetings are sponsored and held at REI meeting rooms and are free by making a reservation through the store web-site.

In the United Kingdom, *The Confraternity of Saint James* (http://www.csj.org.uk) has a vast array of services to assist with plans, maps, books and credentials for pilgrimage to Santiago.

Bibliography

Brierley, John. *A Pilgrim's Guide to the Camino de Santiago.* Forres, Scotland: Findhorn Press Ltd., 2012.

Brierley, John. *A Pilgrim's Guide to the Camino Finisterre.* Forres, Scotland: Findhorn Press Ltd., 2013.

Bryson, Bill. *A Walk in the Woods.* New York, NY: First Anchor Books, 1998.

Belitz, Charlene and Meg Lundstrom. *The Power of Flow.* New York, NY: Three Rivers Press, 1998.

Campbell, Joseph. *The Hero's Journey.* New York, NY: Harper & Row, Publishers, 1990

Campbell, Joseph. *The Power of Myth.* New York, NY: First Anchor Books Edition, 1988.

Chardin, Pierre Teilhard De. *Human Energy.* London, UK: William Collins Sons & Co. Ltd., 1969.

Chatwin, Bruce. *The Songlines.* London, UK: Jonathan Cape, 1987.

Coelho, Paulo. *The Pilgrimage.* San Francisco: Harper San Francisco, 1995.

Cousineau, Phil. The Art of Pilgrimage: San Francisco, CA: Conari Press, 1998

Csikszentmihalyi, Mihaly. *Flow, the Psychology of Optimal Experience.* New York, NY: Harper & Row, 1990.

Dalrymple, William. *From The Holy Mountain.* New York, NY: Henry Holt & Co., Inc. 1997.

Dyer, Wayne W. Change Your Thoughts, Change Your Life. Carlsbad, CA: Hay House, 2007.

Freeman, Philip. *The Philosopher and the Druids.* New York, NY: Simon & Schuster, 2006.

Gibran, Kahil. *The Collected Works*. New York, NY: Borzoi Book/ Alfred A Knopf, 2007.

Gitlitz, David M. and Davidson, Linda Kay. *The Pilgrimage Road to Santiago*. New York, NY: St. Martin's Press, 2000.

Kaku, Michio. *Physics of the Future*. New York, NY: First Anchor Books, 2011.

Louv, Richard. *The Nature Principle*. Chapel Hill, NC: Algonquin Books of Chapel Hill, 2011

MacLaine, Shirley. *The Camino, a Journey of the Spirit*. New York, NY: Pocket Books, 2000

Menocal, María Rosa. *The Ornament of the World*. New York, NY: Back Bay Books / Little brown & Co., 2002

O'Donohue, John. *Anam Cara, a Book of Celtic Wisdom*. New York, NY: Cliff Street Books/ Harper Collins, 1997.

Solnit, Rebecca. *Wanderlust, a History of Walking*. London, UK: Verso, 2001.

Strayed, Cheryl. *Wild, From Lost to Found on the Pacific Crest Trail*. New York, NY: Alfred A. Knopf, 2012.

Tolkien, J. R. R. *The Lord of the Rings*. London, UK: Harper Collins Publishers, 1991. (©1965).

Tolle, Eckhart. *The Power of Now, a Guide to Spiritual Enlightenment*. Novato, CA: New World Library, 1999.

Zukav, Gary. *The Dancing Wu Li Masters*. New York, NY: Harper Collins Publisher, 1979.